Geoff Barton

Active Grammar

OXFORD
UNIVERSITY PRESS

OXFORD

UNIVERSITY PRESS

Great Clarendon Street, Oxford OX2 6DP

Oxford University Press is a department of the University of Oxford.
It furthers the University's objective of excellence in research, scholarship,
and education by publishing worldwide in

Oxford New York

Athens Auckland Bangkok Bogotá Buenos Aires Cape Town
Chennai Dar es Salaam Delhi Florence Hong Kong Istanbul Karachi
Kolkata Kuala Lumpur Madrid Melbourne Mexico City Mumbai Nairobi
Paris São Paulo Shanghai Singapore Taipei Tokyo Toronto Warsaw
with associated companies in Berlin Ibadan

Oxford is a registered trade mark of Oxford University Press
in the UK and in certain other countries

A CIP catalogue record for this book is available from the British Library

ISBN 0-19-831482-5

Designed and typeset by Mike Brain Graphic Design Limited, Oxford

Printed in Spain by Edelvives, Zaragoza

Orders and enquiries to Customer Services:
Tel: 01536 741068   Fax: 01536 454519

Contents

Section Two: Exploring Paragraphs   91

Section Three: Word-level Activities and Reference   123

Active Grammar Glossary   133

Introduction: to the Teacher

This is intended as a new kind of grammar book. It has been written to be fast-paced, interactive and fun, with lots of discussion, problem-solving, rewriting and debating. The idea is that students learn about language in a very active way, through *doing* rather than passively absorbing information. As I wrote it, I was particularly aiming to create a grammar book that would motivate boys, and improve their writing skills. Hence the emphasis on fast-paced, rapidly changing active tasks, with plenty of group work and structured talk.

Most grammar books are fairly passive, designed to show students how to spot a noun phrase or how to admire a famous writer's sentence construction.

Active Grammar isn't like that.

It's rooted in wanting pupils to become better, more reflective writers. It isn't, therefore, based solely on reading skills (most grammar books are). Instead, it moves through reading into writing. It gets students playing around with text, reconstructing it and working out rules and conventions.

Many grammar books use language which feels different from the language pupils encounter outside the classroom. To get examples that fit grammatical rules (sentences containing subjects and verbs, for example) you'd have to ignore a lot of advertising slogans. That can make grammar books feel rarefied, detached from the messy and exciting world of real texts.

This book uses real texts from real contexts, and gets students exploring them in ways that are likely to lead to unpredictable, lively discussion points about structure and effect. This is very much the model of the National Literacy Strategy and the *Framework for English Years 7–9*.

The National Literacy Strategy

Active Grammar takes the sentence-level, text-level and some of the word-level objectives of the Key Stage 3 literacy framework, and builds a sequence of activities around them. The idea is to teach pupils about language features which will then improve their own writing.

There is a strong sense of progression built into each unit. They begin with small-scale language investigations, usually based on reading a sentence or paragraph. They build pupils' skills through a number of rapid activities. Then they move into more developed, written work. In most units, therefore, pupils should progress from reading to writing and from dependence on the book to a real sense of independent writing.

Active Grammar has a consistent structure throughout, one that I've road-tested with my own classes:

Exploring language

Start with a problem, an activity, a language challenge. Move pupils rapidly through, so they feel a sense of development.

Core knowledge

Then consolidate those activities by emphasizing some language principles and conventions. These panels – clearly flagged and dealing with central ideas – are essential for revision and reference.

Practising the skill

The knowledge is then extended into longer, more developed and more ambitious activities, all of them again active and challenging.

Active writing

This is the final consolidation activity – it may be designing a poster, producing a display, generating language guidelines for other classes, rewriting a text . . . They are ideal activities for homework, designed so that pupils embed what they have learnt in their own writing.

Active reading

To be successful, pupils need also to see how other writers are using sentence- and text-level features, so there are a number of Active Reading tasks. These take specific literacy skills and knowledge and get students exploring them in the context of different texts. They aren't passive comprehension questions, but ways of encouraging pupils to investigate writers' language choices.

Word-level features

Active Grammar is chiefly about text- and sentence-level language features, but there are some word-level points which fit neatly into the structure, and these have been included in Section Three. They are designed to improve the accuracy of students' writing.

Timings

One unusual feature is that we've included logos to indicate the kind of pace needed for each activity. Effective grammar teaching is about style as much as content – to be active, lively and entertaining, it needs careful pacing. The logos give you a loose indication of the kind of time envisaged for each activity:

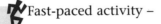

Fast-paced activity –   often spotting features, brainstorming, interrogating sentences

Medium-paced activity –   often exploring features of a text, categorizing, exploring conventions

Slower-paced activity –   usually more reflective, more analytical and involving more extended writing.

This feature is designed to help you sense the necessary pace and timings of activities. It is not, of course, intended as a strait-jacket.

Web support

Some of these activities will work especially well if pupils can have the text in front of them to work on directly, either on a photocopiable page or (ideally) on screen. The *Active Grammar* website (the address is www.oup.com/uk/activegrammar) has lots of the core texts ready to download, plus further hints and activities for pupils.

You might download the materials to your school network or – with some pupils – point them at the site, set the tasks as homework, and leave them to get on with it.

Active teaching hints

I'm hoping pupils will enjoy using this book. I've tested every part of it with my own classes and reshaped it, based on their feedback. In using the materials I've noticed that there are some key ingredients to making it work at its best in the classroom:

◆ First, *teach* from the book. It raises issues for discussion and debate. It has texts which need to be read aloud. It won't work if students are given it to work on in silence, say as a cover lesson. They need to be doing things – talking, reading and writing, in pairs and groups. Make it an active, whole-class experience.

◆ Keep the pace up. The activities are short and punchy. Get pupils working rapidly. Set them short time-limits: 'Four minutes to complete this activity; then let's see what you've found out.'

◆ Remember that this is about 'how to write' as much as it is about grammar. Therefore keep linking language features to effect: Why does the writer choose that pronoun? How would the text be different with simple sentences at that point? Try taking all the adjectives out of that sentence: what's the effect? Pupils therefore get to see that language decisions are not some mysterious gift of great writers, but conscious decisions which have an impact on the text.

◆ Don't worry about repetition. If pupils are to improve their writing, they need to internalize some essential skills – for example, understanding about different sentence types. You won't achieve this in a single lesson. Activities are therefore designed to build, refine, and consolidate their active understanding.

◆ Get involved. There are points when you'll need to roll up your sleeves and do some modelling – that is, use a board or OHP to rework a text with pupils, rewriting it to their suggestions.

◆ Create a literacy-rich room. The activities in the book will generate lots of lists, posters, leaflets, sets of rules. Keep pasting them up around the classroom. Display sentences and paragraphs with clear, easy-to-read annotations by pupils showing their language features. In this way the sterile distinction between language and literature will disappear, in a room full of texts, with pupils' active responses surrounding them.

Conclusion

This has been a fascinating book to write because it's led me to a different teaching style from the one I developed when I first trained. That has perhaps been the key lesson of the NLS – that teaching writing successfully needs a very active approach.

I hope you'll agree that *Active Grammar* gives you that, along with resources and activities which will help your pupils to become better writers.

GEOFF BARTON

Exploring Sentences

Using sentences is probably the most important skill you need in order to do well in English.

Successful writers not only use clear, interesting sentences. They also pay attention to the rhythm of sentences in a text, using simple and complex sentences, detail and brevity, to catch and hold our interest.

This section:

◆ builds your knowledge of sentence types
◆ shows you how to create more interesting texts by adding variety to your sentences
◆ lets you explore the sentence styles of established writers
◆ lets you practise your writing skills in a range of ways.

HOW TO ...
decide what a sentence is

Exploring language

When is a sentence not a sentence?

Look at the groups of words below. They all begin with capital letters and end with full stops . . . but are they sentences?

Activity 1 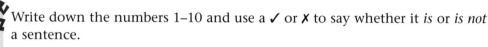 Write down the numbers 1–10 and use a ✓ or ✗ to say whether it *is* or *is not* a sentence.

1 The rat.
2 The rat looks ill.
3 The old fat rat in the porch.
4 The porch needs cleaning.
5 My brother.
6 My brother has broken his arm again.
7 The washing line snapped.
8 The car has.
9 The long fish at the end of the line.
10 The long fish was probably a trout.

Write down how many you think *are* sentences and how many *are not*. Compare your answers with someone else's.

How could you tell which were and which weren't sentences?

Activity 2 Imagine you are talking to someone who is learning language for the first time. He or she doesn't know anything about sentences.

Write down a statement which will tell this language learner what a sentence is. You might start your definition like this:

A sentence is . . .
Or
Sentences are . . .
Or
You can spot a sentence by . . .

Activity 3 Compare your definition with other people in your class.
Vote on which definition seems best to capture what a sentence is.

Activity 4  People will have defined sentences differently. Look at this list of some of the points people might have included. Place them in order of *most* to *least* important:

Sentences . . .

a start with capital letters and end with full stops
b contain a verb
c contain a subject
d make sense
e stand on their own.

Compare how much your group agrees on which are the *most* and *least* important ingredients in sentences.

Core knowledge

Defining what a sentence is should be easy, but in fact it can prove difficult. Most people agree on certain key ingredients:

◆ It must make sense:
   the cat waves on the dream
This is grammatical, but doesn't make sense.

◆ It must stand alone:
   He was.
This doesn't stand alone as a sentence. But in another context it makes sense:
'He wasn't that unkind, was he?' 'He was.'

◆ It must contain a verb:
   Never.
   For a long time.
   On the bus.
These are phrases, rather than sentences.

◆ It contains a subject:
   She sat opposite him
She is the subject.

◆ It is presented in writing with a capital letter at the start and a full stop, exclamation or question mark at the end:
   That's true.

Because language is so powerful, creative and flexible there are exceptions. You may already be able to think of examples which do not contain one or two of these ingredients. You will explore some of these exceptions later.

Practising the skill

Activity 5 In pairs or a group, work on the chart below.

Example	Is it a sentence? If no … main reason?	Y / N	
			a Does not make sense
			b No subject
			c No verb
			d Cannot stand on its own
1 I will never forget that night.			
2 After the storm died down, we were.			
3 The forest was destroyed.			
4 Even the small trees.			
5 A cold wind sang sweet songs through the ugly gloom.			
6 No one could understand why the atmosphere was so strange, but it was.			
7 Nothing stirred.			
8 Absolutely nothing.			
9 We wandered.			
10 Fear in the darkness.			
11 We quickly packed and left.			
12 Never to return.			

Activity 6 Which examples caused most disagreement about whether or not they were sentences?
Why?

Active writing

A

Find examples where writers surprise us by not writing in complete sentences. They might be creating special effects, as in advertising:

Amazing value, amazing quality. Guaranteed.

They may be adding tension or drama to stories:

James looked into the night and saw shapes moving. Moving slowly. Moving closer.

Look for examples in:

◆ books you have read
◆ posters
◆ leaflets
◆ signs
◆ websites
◆ advertising slogans
◆ e-mails.

Find sentences in their work which – placed on their own – don't seem like sentences. Write them down for a display and label them to say why they aren't straightforward sentences.

B

Based on the activities you have done in this unit, write a new definition of what a sentence is.

You might start:

A sentence is . . .
Or
You can spot a sentence by . . .

Try to come up with a definition which will help a new language learner to identify the essential ingredients in sentences.

Compare it with the definition you wrote in Activity 2.
How has your understanding of sentences developed?

2 ACTIVE READING
Simple sentences in children's stories

Simple sentences are ideal for helping children learn to read. They communicate information about one subject using one verb group at a time.

Look at these sentences from *A New Dog*, a book in the Oxford Reading Tree series.

❶ The story currently uses 12 simple sentences.

Use the co-ordinating conjunctions **and**, **but** and **or** to rewrite the story as three or four sentences. Then talk about how the story might feel different for a young reader.

❷ Take sentence 4 and make it into a complex sentence by adding a relative clause about the dogs. A relative clause begins **which** . . . or **that** . . . or **who** . . . Make up some details about the dogs.

Kipper wanted a dog.
Everyone wanted a dog.
They went to the dogs' home.
They looked at the dogs.
Kipper wanted this dog.
It was too big.
Biff wanted this dog.
It was too little.
Mum wanted this dog.
It was too strong.
Everyone liked this dog.
They took the dog home.

❸ Look at the way the writer uses the demonstrative adjective **this** in the phrase **this dog**.

This gives you a clue about the pictures that would be with the sentences. How does **this** tell you that there must be a picture?

❹ Look at sentence 3. Look at the use of the apostrophe in the phrase **the dogs' home**. How would the meaning of the phrase be different if it said **the dog's home**?

Active writing

Imagine the story as the first paragraph of a text for an older audience – say the beginning of a story for teenagers.
◆ How would you rewrite it?
◆ Which words would you change?
◆ How would you change the simple sentences?

Write your new version and, in the margin, use arrows and labels to highlight and explain the main changes you have made.

3 HOW TO ...
create simple sentences

Exploring language

Activity 1 What do you know about your early language?

- When did you say your first word?
- What was it?
- What were the first words of other people in your group?

Activity 2 List the first words spoken by people in your group.
Make links between them – what patterns are there?

For example:

1 How many people say the same words (e.g. dada, mama, ball)?
2 Group the words under topic headings:
   people – food/drink – parts of the body – animals – places
3 What word classes are there? Nouns? Verbs? Pronouns (me)?
   Demonstrative adverbs (there)?
4 Which words do you find difficult to categorize?

Activity 3 Some time after children say their first word, they start to put words together. Then they begin to use simple sentences. At first these may be 'telegrammatic' (leaving out some grammatical words) or ungrammatical (using the pronoun me instead of I). Explore the way children around the age of two begin to use sentence structures.

GLOSSARY

Telegrammatic language

A language style that leaves out some words (grammatical words). Young children use this style when they have mastered their first words but are still unable to speak in complete sentences. It sounds like this:

'Me like Mummy. Me play big ball.'

The child uses **lexical** words (words that carry specific information) and leaves out **grammatical** words (words which provide structure within sentences)

Copy out the table and then:

1 discuss and write down what you think the child might be saying (there could be several possible meanings)
2 expand each example into a grammatical sentence.

Download this resource from the Active Grammar website

Example	What the child might mean (this could be more than one thing, so you may need to expand the example into two or more sentences)
Me want juice.	E.g. I want a drink. E.g. I am thirsty.
1 Daddy home now.	
2 Me no go.	
3 Sam sick.	
4 Car here now.	
5 Me no like this stuff.	

Activity 4 Look again at examples 1 to 5. Decide whether you think each one counts as a sentence or not. Try to say why.

Core knowledge

You can see from these examples that the children are beginning to speak using simple sentences – even if they haven't got them completely right yet.

We usually begin to use simple sentences from around the age of two. They contain a subject, a verb, and make sense on their own.

Simple sentences may be very short:

a The cat has fleas.

Or longer:

b The cat on the neighbouring housing estate has developed a nasty case of flea infection.

Example **b** is much longer than **a**, but it is still a simple sentence because:

◆ It has a single subject (the cat)
◆ It contains a single verb or verb phrase (e.g. has developed)
◆ It makes sense on its own
◆ It is not joined to another clause.

Plus: in writing it has a capital letter at the start and a full stop at the end.

GLOSSARY

Verb phrase

Sometimes we use a number of verbs together to add detail, for example about tense (when something happened).

For example:

I eat
↑
main verb

I have eaten = verb phrase
↑   ↑
auxiliary verb   main verb

I will eat = verb phrase
↑   ↑
auxiliary verb   main verb

 I would have eaten = verb phrase
↑   ↑   ↑
auxiliary verb   auxiliary verb   main verb

Practising the skill

Activity 5  ◆ Which of these examples *are* simple sentences?
◆ Which are not – and why?

1 There was a massive fire at a local paper warehouse just last week.
2 A lot of damage was caused.
3 All through the warehouse.
4 More than 20 firefighters were called to the huge blaze.
5 They battled through the night.
6 Into the early hours.
7 The raging fire was brought under control at around 3 a.m.
8 Calm returned.

Active writing

Many books for young children use simple sentences to teach children to read, like this:

Peter is here. Jane is here. Here they are in the water. They like the water. Here is Pat, the dog. Pat likes the water. Pat likes fun.

These are short simple sentences aimed at helping children to recognize a small number of key words. To an older reader it can feel babyish.

What happens when you use short simple sentences in different contexts?

1 Choose one of the story contexts below.
2 Then write one paragraph using short simple sentences.
3 Then discuss or write about the effect of using short simple sentences in that context. Do they:

◆ Add drama? Make it feel childish? Give impact? Add clarity? Make it easy to follow? Feel repetitive?

Story contexts:
A storm at sea: a small fishing-boat is caught in the middle of it.
Or
An earthquake in a large city: people narrowly escape from a tall tower-block.

Use short simple sentences, as used in the Peter and Jane books, and see what the effect is. You might start like this:
The sea grew wild. The sky was . . .
Or
People screamed. The floor . . .

4 ACTIVE READING
Simple sentences in instructions

Simple sentences can be ideal for writing instructions. They can make information clear to follow.

Look at these sentences from a Sainsbury's leaflet about healthy eating. Most of them are simple sentences. Explore the effect.

❶ Most of the sentences here are simple sentences. Which one is not?

❷ Many of the sentences are imperatives (commands). They begin with the verb – like this:

Look out for . . . Use . . . Try . . .

How could you write those sentences as different sentence functions – for example, statements or questions?

Food ideas and cooking tips

✓ Skimmed and semi-skimmed milks are good choices.

✓ There is a wide range of vegetarian cheeses available. Check the labels for the 'suitable for vegetarians' symbol.

✓ Look out for the Be Good to Yourself range of lower fat cheeses.

✓ Use smaller quantities of strongly flavoured cheeses for cooking.

✓ If you don't eat dairy foods, look out for dairy alternatives fortified with calcium, such as Soya milk, rice milk and other products made with Soya.

✓ Try the Be Good to Yourself crème fraiche or fromage frais as a lower fat alternative to cream.

❸ The writer has used bullet-points. How do these help communicate information?

❹ Do you think the list of simple sentences becomes too repetitive? What would happen if you used a co-ordinating conjunction (**and**, **but** or **or**) to join two of the sentences together?

Try rewriting the first three sentences in one continuous paragraph, using co-ordinating conjunctions to join at least two of the sentences together.

❺ Bullet-point 5 is a different sentence type. Try writing it as two simple sentences.

Active writing

Imagine the text in a different situation. Someone who works for Sainsbury's is talking to a customer and giving advice about diet and healthy eating.

◆ How would the words and sentences be different?

Write a paragraph or two to show how language might be used.

Then use labels and arrows to show the main changes you have made.
You might also be able to label any differences you notice between written and spoken language.

5 HOW TO...
use adjectives, adverbs and phrases to modify simple sentences

Exploring language

Activity 1

Read this simple sentence. It is a statement.

The creature is dying.

Revision

What makes a simple sentence a simple sentence?
◆ It contains one subject.
◆ It contains one verb or verb phrase (e.g. eat or has eaten).
◆ It is not joined up to another clause.
◆ It makes sense on its own.

Q: How could you add more detail to the sentence?
A: You could tell the reader more about *the creature* or about the *way it is dying* or about *where it is*.

Use the sketch and notes below. See if you can add detail to the sentence *without* adding another verb and *without* joining the sentence to another sentence by using and, but or or.

◆ The creature: scaly, green, slimy, stinking
◆ How it is dying: agonizingly, slowly, loudly
◆ Whereabouts: in a ditch, half-submerged in water

Activity 2

Take these three boring sentences. Add some detail to different parts of each sentence. Try to make each sentence more interesting by adding some unexpected details – for example:

The bird is singing

could become

The **ancient**, **battered** bird is singing **croakily in the dying tree**

adjectives   adverb   phrase

See if you can do something similar with these sentences.

The water was rising.
The bike fell.
My sister ran.

Core knowledge

We can add details to simple sentences using a number of techniques:

Adjectives to describe the noun (e.g. slimy + monster)
Phrases to describe place and manner (e.g. in a ditch)
Adverbs to describe the manner of something (e.g. loudly)

Adding features like this to a sentence is known as **modification**.

The sentences are still simple because they have one subject and one verb. But the extra detail makes them more precise and interesting to read.

GLOSSARY

Modification

Modification allows us to add detail to texts. For example, we can:

Modify a noun with an adjective: the **ugly** animal
Modify a noun with a phrase: the animal **in the car park**
Modify a noun with a clause: the animal **which I hated to look at**
Modify an adjective with an adverb: the **very** ugly animal
Modify a verb with an adverb: the house was **slowly** collapsing
Modify a verb with a phrase: the house was collapsing **before our eyes**
Modify a verb with a clause: the house was collapsing, **which I had first noticed at noon**.

Practising the skill

Activity 3   Modifying simple sentences in this way is useful because it can make your sentences more interesting. But you can also be tempted to add too many details.

Take this simple sentence.

The wind was howling.

Add three adjectives about the wind.
Add two adverbs about how the wind howled.
Add a phrase about where it happened (e.g. in the woods) or when (yesterday/last week).

Does your sentence feel too clogged up with details yet?

Add another adjective or adverb or phrase.

Activity 4   Look at the following densely written sentences. Which of them have too much detail in your opinion?

a The cold, grey, damp snow lay sparkling brightly and attractively on the long, flat, barren field.
b Ageing ex-hippy Ron Wallace yesterday bought a large bottle of raspberry-flavoured medicine in his local chemist's shop.
c Happy-go-lucky brain surgeon Veronica Nettleton rested for a moment on her luxury 4-berth yacht off Lowestoft pier near the Magpie chip shop.

Activity 5   Which elements (adjectives, adverbs, phrases) would you edit out of the sentences to make them feel more straightforward?

Activity 6   Based on the last activity, what would your advice be to new writers? Complete these statements:

1 In general the maximum number of adjectives you should use to modify a noun is ___. The maximum number of adverbs to modify an adverb is ____.

2 Some texts are suitable for lots of modification, such as _____.
3 Some texts are less suitable for lots of modification, such as _____ _____.

Choose from these texts: newspapers, autobiographies, recipes, websites, poems, stories, police reports, instructions.

Active writing

Now look at this very boring scene from a children's story. The simple sentences make it seem very basic and rather childish. The arrows show places where you could add detail to try to make the description more vivid.

Use adjectives, phrases and adverbs to liven it up – without putting in so much description that the story feels clogged up. To add more description, think of words and phrases that will answer these questions:

- ◆ Which?
- ◆ Where?
- ◆ How?
- ◆ When?

Mystery at Murky Water

The ↗ pond was ↗ deep. There were ↗ shadows. The water was ↗ green. The ↗ children looked ↗ at it. There was no ↗ sound. It was getting ↗ dark. Dave heard a sound. It was ↗ soft. He listened ↗. It was a ↗ rustling. It got ↗ louder. The ↗ children looked ↗ at each other. A ↗ fish jumped ↗. They turned ↗. Behind them was a man. He looked ↗ angry …

Here are some ways that you could make the first sentence more interesting:

- ◆ The old pond was deep (add adjective *old*)
- ◆ The pond was very deep (add adverb *very*)
- ◆ The pond beneath the trees was worryingly deep (add phrase *beneath the trees* and adverb *worryingly*)
- ◆ The pond seemed deep (change verb to *seemed*).

1 Produce your rewritten version.
2 Compare it with what other people have written.
3 Now write the next paragraph of the story. You might want this one to contain dialogue or action rather than more description.

6 ACTIVE READING
Exploring modification

Gervase Phinn was a school inspector in North Yorkshire. His books describe the people and places he saw.

Look more closely at the way he uses modification to bring the scenes to life.

THE OTHER SIDE OF THE DALE

County Hall was a large, grey, stone mansion of an edifice built to last. It stood like many a Yorkshire town hall, sturdy and imposing, and dominating the centre of the market town of Fettlesham. Surrounding it were formal gardens with well-tended lawns and neat footpaths. The interior was like a museum, hushed and cool, with long echoey, oak-panelled corridors, high ornate ceilings, marble figures and walls full of gilt-framed portraits of former councillors, mayors, aldermen, leaders of the Council, high sheriffs, lord lieutenants, members of parliament and other dignitaries. It was really quite a daunting place.

Gervase Phinn

❶ Find an example of the writer using two or more adjectives to modify a noun.

❷ Take one sentence and rewrite it without any modification. Describe how the new sentence feels different.

❸ Find an example of the way the writer uses a simile (comparing things using the linking words **as** or **like**).

❹ The writer uses a lot of adjectives. Classify them according to the senses they refer to. Which adjectives are related to:
- sight
- sound
- feeling?

Active writing

Rewrite the text to appear in a factual guide book about County Hall.

Think about:

◆ The tense (will you use past or present tense?)
◆ The amount of description (will you change the amount of modification?)

Write a factual paragraph about County Hall.

7 HOW TO ...
create compound sentences

Exploring language

Activity 1  How long does it take before a text written only in simple sentences becomes boring? Read this ten-sentence text. At which sentence do you think its style becomes repetitive and dull?

Mobile phones are a menace **1**. They drive me mad **2**. Some people use them all the time **3**. Obviously they use them for phone calls **4**. They can also use them for text messages **5**. Many phones also feature games **6**. It is all very annoying **7**. These people should talk to people instead **8**. They should make human contact **9**. Mobile phones are destroying real communication **10**.

Compare your thoughts with other people in your group as to how quickly the text style becomes too repetitive.

Activity 2 Look at this comment on the ten-sentence paragraph:

'Of course the paragraph is boring. It isn't just because of the simple sentences; it's because the choice of words is so dull. Look at how many times the writer uses the verbs "is/are" and "use". Just by changing these you could make the paragraph more interesting.'

Do you agree?

Think of synonyms (words with the same meaning) for *are* and *use*. You might use phrases instead of single words. Here are some examples:

are	use
seem	make use of
can be	utilize
may be	employ
prove	rely on

a Now see if the paragraph becomes more interesting when you use some of those synonyms to replace the boring vocabulary.
b Which of the synonyms make the text seem too formal?

Activity 3   Even if improving the vocabulary has some effect, the string of ten simple sentences reads too much like a list. Choose two or three of the sentences and join them together using these conjunctions:

and
but
or

Read the paragraph through again. How has adding these conjunctions improved the text?

Core knowledge

Sentences can be joined together using conjunctions *and*, *or* or *but*. This makes simple sentences into compound (or co-ordinated) sentences. For example:

Two simple sentences . . .
Mobile phones are a menace. They drive me mad.

. . . can become one compound sentence:
Mobile phones are a menace and they drive me mad.

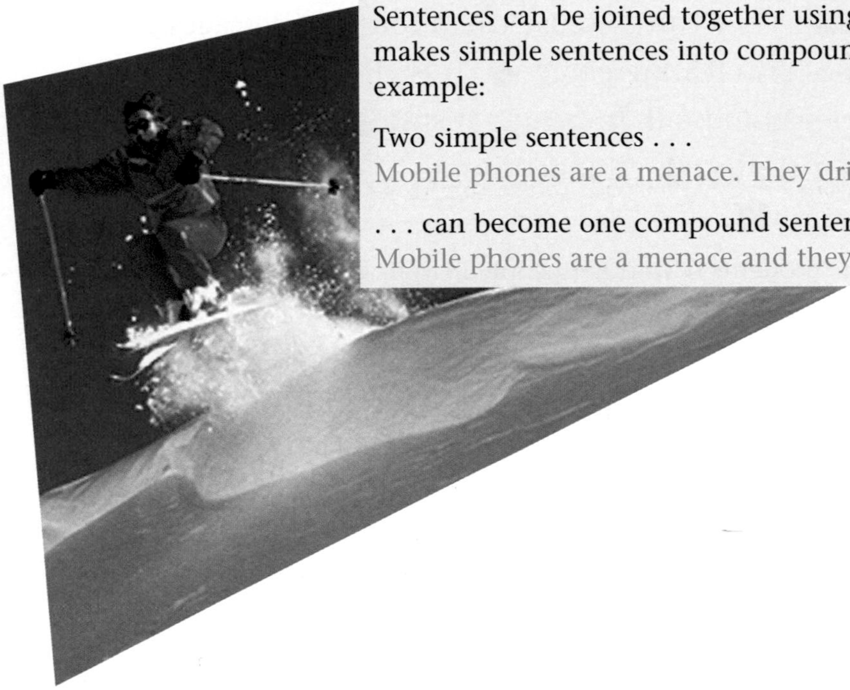

Practising the skill

Activity 4   Take these pairs of simple sentences and make them into compound sentences using *and*, *but* or *or*.

1 The clouds look dark. It might rain.
2 The rain seems heavy. There is bright sky ahead.
3 You could stay indoors. You could go outside.
4 It's certainly warm in here. We'll have to leave eventually.
5 I used to hate wet weather. I thought I did.

Activity 5

In Activity 4, how did you decide whether to use *and*, *but* or *or*? Could you have used any of the three co-ordinators?

Choose *one* of the topics below. Write down three compound sentences of your own – one using *and*, one using *but*, and one using *or*. Write all three of your sentences on your chosen topic. Use the sentence models to get you started, if you wish.

Topics

◆ A visit to town – describe which shops you went to.
◆ Something that happened on the way to school this morning.
◆ A description of the classroom you are in at the moment.

Sentence models

Last week I . . . and/but/or I . . .
Today my friend . . . and/but/or the bus . . .
The room is . . . and/but/or it is . . .

Activity 6

How are the conjunctions *and*, *but* and *or* different in their meanings? Can you use any of them in any sentence? Try these sentences:

The driver looks angry. There is a crash further along the road.

Try adding *and*, *but* and *or* between the two simple sentences. That will give you three new compound sentences

Can you think of any context where you could use each of the new sentences, or do they sound wrong?

Activity 7

In theory you could use the conjunctions *and*, *but* and *or* to join simple sentences together endlessly. You sometimes find young children do this . . .

I am four and my sister is three and she is often cross but today she is happy and we are going for a picnic but I am taking my bucket and spade and we will play on the beach but not if it's raining and then we will come home and I will watch Tweenies and . . .

George

George, age 4

Take George's long compound sentence. Make it more controlled by breaking it into several shorter sentences. Leave some sentences as compound sentences and make others into simple sentences.

Rewrite his paragraph for him so that it becomes clearer for a reader to follow.

Activity 8   Compare your rewriting of George's sentence with a friend's. How have you combined simple and compound sentences differently?

Activity 9   Some writers say it is good style to use simple sentences at the start and end of a paragraph, with compound sentences in the middle. They say it can make factual writing much clearer. Do you agree?

Choose one of these topics and write a paragraph in this way:

1 simple sentence
3 compound sentences
1 simple sentence

Instructions on
◆ mending a bicycle puncture
◆ cleaning a hamster's cage
◆ making a cup of tea.

Activity 10  Does the sentence formula make your instructions clear?
Compare your paragraph with a friend's. Do your paragraphs feel similar because they use the same pattern of sentence types?

Active writing

A

Put together a poster about simple and compound sentences aimed at other people taught in your classroom.

Explain:

a what these sentence types are
b give advice on how they work best.

B

Find examples of simple and compound sentences in books. Write them out. Label them. Display them around your classroom.

8 ACTIVE READING
Compound sentences in children's stories

Compound sentences can go on forever. They join clauses together with *and*, *but* or *or* and – in theory – you could keep a sentence going until you run out of ink or breath.

Children's stories often use simple sentences. But they also use compound sentences to create a different effect. Look at this example from *Sailor Bear* by Martin Waddell and Virginia Austin.

❶ Look at the compound sentence **He thought and he thought**. Try reading the story with this as a simple sentence: **He thought**. What is the effect of repeating **thought**?

❷ Look at the second sentence on page 2. It starts with the conjunction **But**. Why do you think the writer has started the sentence like this? How would it be different if the writer:
a joined the sentence to the previous one?
b deleted the conjunction and started the sentence with **He**?

PAGE 1

Sailor Bear was a bear in a sailor suit who was lost and had no one to play with. 'Now what shall I do?' wondered Small Bear.

 He thought and he thought. Then he looked at his suit and he knew what to do.

PAGE 2

'I'll be a sailor, and sail on the sea!' decided Small Bear.

 But he hadn't a boat.

 'Now what shall I do?' wondered Small Bear.

 He thought and he thought. Then he looked at the sea and he knew what to do.

❸ Like many children's books, *Sailor Bear* uses a lot of repetition. Look at the storyline for page 3. See if you can predict what the page will say.

Storyline (page 3):
• Small Bear decides to go and get a boat
• They are too big
• He looks round the shore.

❹ Compare your page with the text other people have written.

❺ Why do you think repetition like this might be helpful for young children?

Active writing

The story uses a variety of sentence structures, including compound sentences. How would it sound if it used only simple sentences?

◆ Write the text out in simple sentences.
◆ Write a sentence describing how different the story feels when written in this way.

HOW TO ...
create complex sentences

Exploring language

Activity 1 How many ways can you find of joining up these pairs of simple sentences *without* using *and*, *but* or *or*? Don't be tempted to join sentences together using commas!

a I went to see the doctor. She gave me some tablets.
b I enjoyed the visit to the castle. It was really unpleasant in there.
c I had finished my homework. I watched TV.
d I noticed the man. He was reading a newspaper.

Activity 2 With a friend, look at the different ways you joined sentences together. Try to sort them into these categories:

◆ Adding new linking words (but not *and*, *but* or *or*)
◆ Changing the structure of sentences to join the two parts together.

Activity 3 We usually expect conjunctions to go between the sentences you want to join, like this:

Catherine visited my auntie **when** she came to the UK.

Think of two or three other conjunctions or phrases that you could put instead of when.

Activity 4 Some conjunctions can go in front of the sentences you are joining, like this:

Although Catherine was in a hurry, she visited my auntie.

Copy out these words and use a ✓ or ✗ to show which of these words *could* and *could not* replace although:

because
whenever
despite
even though
however
whilst

Activity 5 You can use the relative pronouns *who*, *which*, and *that* to join simple sentences together, like this:

Pete was my mother's schoolfriend. He visited yesterday.

becomes

Pete, **who** was my mother's schoolfriend, visited yesterday.

The sentence now has two clauses – a main clause, which gives the main information (Pete visited yesterday) and a relative clause, which gives background information (who was my mother's schoolfriend).

Try matching up some of these main clauses and relative clauses to come up with some complex sentences. Aim to make your examples as lively as possible.

Download this resource from the Active Grammar website

Try adding a relative clause here . . . or here

Take a . . . main clause	Add a . . . relative pronoun	And add a . . . relative clause
The bats ✳ were hanging in the cave ✳	that	my auntie bought in a car-boot sale
The old poodle was sniffing around the dustbin	that	was a shame
The best man's speech suddenly ended	which	was really smelly
The butcher dropped a large sausage on to the counter	who	had knobbly knees
		was overflowing with rubbish
		was really disappointing
		was covered in blood
		was known as Greasy Gary
		was far too long
		had escaped from the back of a car
		scared me to death

GLOSSARY

Relative clause

A group of words built around a verb, which you can add to sentences to give more detail.

Take a simple sentence: My dog is looking unwell.
Add a relative clause after the subject: My dog, which was four last week, is looking unwell.

You can add relative clauses at other points, too: My dog is looking unwell, which is a shame.

Activity 6 Think of some more wacky sentences which use main clauses and relative clauses. Look back at Activity 5 to get some ideas.

Activity 7 Think of some rules to explain how we know whether to use the relative pronouns who, which or that. Start like this:

Use 'who' when . . .
Use 'which' when . . .
Use 'that' when . . .

Core knowledge

Using complex sentences in your writing can really improve your written style.

You can create complex sentences in a number of ways:

a Use conjunctions between clauses:

Until	He kept playing **until** everyone had left the room.
Although	He kept playing **although** no one was listening.
Before	He kept playing **before** finally giving up.
Since	He kept playing **since** they were paying him well.

b Use conjunctions at the start of sentences:

Although everyone had left the room, he kept playing.
Because everyone had left the room, he stopped playing.
Even though no one was listening, he kept playing.

c Use relative pronouns to pack more information into a sentence:

The piano, **which** had been tuned that morning, was in perfect condition.
The piano was in perfect condition, **which** made a nice change.
The music **that** he brought was pretty basic.
The boss **who** paid him seemed happy enough.

Practising the skill

Activity 8  The grid below gives a lot of information about a subject. From these facts, different types of sentences could be made about the subject.

Subject	Information
My uncle	42
	very funny
	works in an office
	broke his leg skiing last year

Here are some examples.

a Simple sentence version:
◆ My 42-year-old uncle is very funny. He works in an office. He went skiing last year. He broke his leg.

b Compound sentence version:
◆ My 42-year-old uncle is very funny and he works in an office, and he went skiing last year but he broke his leg.

c Complex sentence version:
◆ My 42-year-old uncle, who is very funny and works in an office, broke his leg skiing last year.

◆ Which sounds most like spoken English?
◆ Which sounds most like a report?
◆ Which sounds best?

Activity 9 Practise writing the three sentence types yourself.

Download this resource from the Active Grammar website

For each subject below, write a simple sentence version, a compound sentence version, and a complex sentence version – as in Activity 8.

1 Subject Mr Hall	**Information** 41 teacher born in Harrogate never loses his temper
2 Subject The wind	**Information** fierce very cold started blowing this morning before daylight will probably carry on all day
3 Subject Annette	**Information** 14 away from school today feeling ill with stomach ache feels worse after watching daytime television
4 Subject The water	**Information** just poured from the jug bit murky has a small worm floating in it
5 Subject The computer	**Information** just bought showing strange behaviour screen keeps freezing probably has a problem with the hard drive needs to go back to the supplier

Activity 10   Look at the range of different sentences you have written.

a Which is the best complex sentence? Why?

b Which examples – if any – work better as simple or compound sentences?

Activity 11   When do complex sentences begin to get overloaded with information? Is it possible to spoil them by cramming in too many details?

Try making a complex sentence from this:

Subject	Information
My sister	Jane
	12
	likes music
	has a best friend called Lisa
	has gone into town this afternoon
	hoping to buy a new CD
	worried she can't afford it
	asked if she could borrow money from me
	I said – only if you pay me interest

Is it impossible to get all this information into one sentence?

Activity 12   Write three bullet-points giving advice to pupils in another class, advising them how to use complex sentences:

◆ Explain what a complex sentence is
◆ Say what complex sentences are good for
◆ Give advice on how best to use them.

Active writing

Read this text on the subject of the Olympics.

At the moment it is written in a monotonous style, with too many simple sentences.

Rewrite it to make it more interesting. Use the techniques you have learned in this unit so that you are creating some complex sentences.

The Olympic Games are very old. The Greek Olympics started in 776 BC. They were ended in AD 393 by the Emperor Theodosius. He did not approve of the games. They were not religious enough for him. Some early games were highly dangerous. The worst was the pankration. This was a duel between two men. It was a duel to the death. The game was later banned. Gouging, limb-breaking and strangulation were still permitted, though. Only men of pure Greek descent took part in the Olympics. Women were not allowed to watch. They were sometimes thrown off a cliff.

10 HOW TO...
spot co-ordination and subordination

Exploring language

Activity 1 Look at these sentences. Each has two halves. For each sentence decide which is the main message of the sentence, and which is the background information. The first one is done for you:

After arriving home, Sam watched some TV.

↑ Background information   ↑ Main message

1 Despite feeling quite ill, he stayed up for an hour.
2 He ate a sandwich, even though he was unwell.
3 He watched *Friends*, which he usually enjoyed.
4 Finally he went to bed because it was so late.

Activity 2 Try to spot background information and main message in these slightly more complex sentences:

1 Chloe worked at the supermarket, something she usually enjoyed.
2 Although she had worked there for over a year now, she still quite liked the job.
3 In a year's time, after taking her final exams, she would be going to university.
4 The part-time job, which she did for eight hours a week, would provide important cash.
5 Finishing work at 6 p.m., she phoned her friends.

Activity 3 Now look at these **compound** sentences. See if it is possible with these to identify the main message and background information.

Reminder:
Compound sentences use the conjunctions *and*, *but*, and *or* to join clauses together.

1 Sian finished her homework and went into the garden.
2 It had been sunny earlier but was now starting to rain.
3 She needed some fresh air but hated the rain.
4 She went back inside and put on a CD.
5 She would either read a book or look through a magazine or just do nothing.

Core knowledge

Compound and complex sentences contain more than one clause.

In **compound sentences** these are joined by the conjunctions and, but, and or. Each clause is co-ordinated with the next. This means that each clause is as important as the next – like this:

I saw the car and then it disappeared.

Two clauses
co-ordinated by conjunction and
both clauses are equally important (neither is background information)

In **complex sentences**, clauses can be joined in different ways. One clause will be the main clause, the other will be the subordinate clause.

◆ The main clause carries the main message of the sentence.
◆ The subordinate clause carries the background information.
◆ There may be several subordinate clauses.

Example:

Walking along the country lane, I noticed the car.

Two clauses
◆ the initial -ing clause gives background information (what I was doing when the main event happened) – it is therefore the subordinate clause
◆ main clause

Here are other ways of writing the sentence.

I noticed the car as I was walking down the lane.
I noticed the car because I was walking down the lane.
I noticed the car when I walked down the lane.
I noticed the car which was parked down the lane.

There are different kinds of background information here, but the main clause remains the same – I noticed the car.

Practising the skill

Activity 4 Decide whether these sentences use co-ordination or subordination and label them **C** or **S**:

1 I saw the dog and I ran for cover.
2 Hiding behind the wall, I waited for a second.
3 All seemed quiet but I stayed there.
4 The dog, which belonged to a neighbour, seemed to be moving away.
5 I was still too afraid to move and I stayed put.
6 The dog shuffled down the street, hardly paying attention to anyone now.
7 I stepped out from behind the wall, still feeling nervous.
8 The dog paused, or at least I thought he did.

Active writing

Choose one of the topics below and write a paragraph which uses co-ordinated and subordinated clauses. Write the paragraph in the middle of the page. Around the edge put labels and arrows to show your reader what type of sentence each one is, like this:

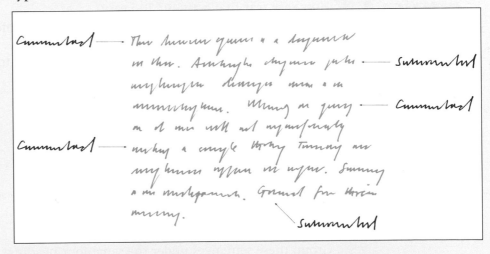

Topics

◆ Describe your journey to school this morning
◆ Imagine you were once terrified by an animal – e.g. dog, rat, spider

HOW TO ...
identify sentence functions

Exploring language

Activity 1

Sentences come in different types.
Look at the groups of words below. Sort them out under these headings:

questions   statements   commands   non-sentences

◆ Is this my meal?
◆ It's not hot.
◆ Well –
◆ Warm it up, please.
◆ Throw it away then.
◆ It looks uncooked.
◆ Where is the manager?
◆ I said –
◆ I'm leaving.

Activity 2

How easy was that activity? Too easy?
Think about how you worked out what types of sentences each word group was.
How important was the punctuation? Is it possible to spot sentence types even when there is no punctuation?
Try these:

◆ the cat probably ate it
◆ where did you leave it
◆ move that out of the way
◆ stop crying
◆ she enjoyed the jokes
◆ the cushion on the floor
◆ the noise is driving me mad

Group these sentences under the same four headings:

questions   statements   commands   non-sentences

Then think about the *main clue* that helped you to identify what type of sentence it was.

Activity 3

Now write four statements for a new language learner, explaining how to spot different types of sentences. Start your definitions like this:

1 *You can spot a question by . . .*
2 *You can spot a statement by . . .*
3 *You can spot a command by . . .*
4 *You can spot a non-sentence because . . .*

Core knowledge

Simple sentences have certain key ingredients, and by moving these around we can create different sentence types.

Key ingredients:
Simple sentences contain a *subject*.
This is the person, animal or thing who is doing something.

They contain a single *verb*.
This is the action that the subject is doing.

Statements usually put the subject before the verb, like this:
The man was moody.
The politician has resigned.

Questions usually put the verb (or part of the verb) in front of the subject – for example:
Was the man moody?
Has the politician resigned?

Sometimes they add a question word (who . . . which . . . what . . . why . . . when)
When **did** the politician resign?
Why **was** the man moody?

Commands usually place the verb right at the start of the sentence and can leave out the subject:
Sit down.
Lift that up.

Non-sentences will usually have the verb missing:
The man.
Underneath the chestnut tree.

GLOSSARY

Sentence functions and sentence types

Sentence functions indicate the purposes of sentences: **statements, questions, commands** and **exclamations**.
Sentence types are **simple, compound** and **complex**.

Practising the skill

Activity 4

These different sentences can be useful in different types of texts.

Questions are important for finding out information. They can also be useful for getting a reader involved in a text – like this:

Why am I a vegetarian? Eating meat is wrong. It is cruel and unfair to animals. It leads to factory farming. How would you like to live without sunlight? How would you like to be locked in a cage all day? It is an appalling way to treat any creature.

Look at this text and notice how the mixture of **statements** and **questions** gives power to the writing.

Questions used like this are called **rhetorical questions**. They are questions designed to make the reader think about your message.

Activity 5

Practising statements and questions

Choose one of the topics below and practise writing your own mix of statements and questions.

Why the Internet is a good/bad thing; *or*
Why school uniform is a sensible/foolish idea

Statements might start like this:
◆ *The Internet is . . . Many people use . . . Various websites are . . .*

Questions might start like this:
◆ *Would you allow . . .?*
◆ *Should children have . . .?*

Activity 6   Practising commands

Commands can be used in various contexts. Sometimes they are formal and sometimes informal, sometimes very direct, sometimes polite:

Sit down now!
Have a cup of coffee.
Take a tablet.

Make up some signs for your classroom. Make some of them abrupt, and others very polite. Try to give the same message using different tones.

Example:

Always shut the window.
Please always remember to close the window.
Please try to close the window behind you if possible.

Write five more signs in different tones.
Compare other people's signs.
Which are the key ingredients in making the tone more or less polite?

Activity 7   Practising commands

Commands can be useful in instructional writing – for example, in recipes:
First take an egg. Separate the white from the yolk. Whisk the whites until stiff.

Write a set of simple sentence commands to help someone new to your school get from your present classroom to the main reception.

Activity 8  **Practising statements**

Statements are useful for factual writing and for giving opinions. But they can become very repetitive when they are just simple sentences.

Remember: a simple sentence has one subject and one verb. This makes them fairly short:

I like cheese.
That car is driving too fast.
The rain is expected later today.

Simple sentence statements are excellent for making yourself clear. But look what happens if you write a whole text in that style:

This computer seems broken. The mouse is not working. The screen seems to have frozen. I need some advice. I will find a technician.

The style can feel very like the books we used when we were learning to read:

Here is Jane. She looks happy. Here is Peter. He is having fun.

Simple sentence statements can create a childlike effect. Write the opening paragraph of a new fairy story using only simple sentence statements. Your characters:

The magic hamster
◆ A poor boy called Ralph with a wicked auntie
◆ A magic hamster called Trevor who helps him escape

You could start like this:
Ralph was sad. He was always sad . . .

Activity 9 Now look at what happens to your story if you add in questions and commands.
Rewrite your first paragraph varying the style more.
For example, you could use rhetorical questions:
Do you know what he saw?
Will I ever escape?

Or add a command:
Sweep up.
Stop wasting time.

Example:
Do you know what he saw? A large cat was moving towards him. 'Stop!' he cried out. The cat ignored him.

Use a similar mix of sentences to rewrite your own first paragraph.

Activity 10 **Practising non-sentences**

In general we write in sentences. But sometimes writers use non-sentences (called minor sentences) to create a special effect, such as adding emphasis to their message – like this:

Don't walk into those woods again. **Ever.**
You haven't eaten breakfast? **Really?**
This recipe needs mushrooms. **Any mushrooms.**

Spot the minor sentences in this text. They are the sentences without verbs:
Web Magic can help you today. A website for you. For your business. For all your needs. Phone Web Magic today.

Writing in non-sentences can be risky. Examiners and teachers might think you can't write in sentences. You can usually avoid using non-sentences through punctuation, like this:

Don't walk into those woods again – **ever.**
You haven't eaten breakfast – **really?**
This recipe needs mushrooms, **any mushrooms.**

Think of some advertising slogans for the product below, using some minor sentences.

Plum Computers: think of a slogan to say that they are the fastest and most powerful computers on the planet. Use a minor sentence. Then write the same idea using a simple or complex sentence. What different effects do they create?

Active writing

Choose one of the topics below and write three paragraphs in which you use statements, commands, questions, plus one non-sentence for effect. At the moment, don't worry if it seems a bit too straightforward.

Topics:
◆ Your opinion of using the Internet
◆ A factual account of what your school looks like
◆ A report about a band or singer you love or loathe

Use this structure to get you started:
◆ Start with some statements to give your opinion.
◆ Then use a question to involve the reader. (Is this fair? Does that make sense?)
◆ Return to statements.
◆ Finish with a command. (Try it yourself. Listen to them today. Visit soon.)

Then see if there's one point where you might want to use a non-sentence to add emphasis – for example, by repeating a word on its own, or a phrase:

Listen to them soon. Very soon.

12 ACTIVE READING
Using minor sentences for special effects

Since you started learning to write, you will probably have been told that sentences must contain a verb.

Usually that is true. But writers sometimes wish to create special effects by using sentences without verbs – 'minor sentences'.

Here is an example from cookery writer Nigel Slater. Look at the effects he creates by placing major and minor sentences side by side.

❶ Take example A. Write it as one complete sentence.

❷ Now write it as two sentences.

❸ Why do you think Nigel Slater has written it as three sentences? What effect does that structure have?

A
I do bake my own bread as it happens. At least once a year. And always in the spring.

B
I barely worked for my lunch, picking from the most prolific vegetable garden I have ever encountered. A garden lush with rows of broad beans, baby beets, waving carrot fronds, chicory, chard and corn. There were aubergines and peppers under glass and, of course, tomatoes. But best of all there were peas.

❹ Look at example B. It consists of four sentences, structured like this:

1: complex
2: minor
3: simple
4: simple

How would you make the minor sentence into a simple sentence?

❺ Look at sentence 4. Why do you think the writer starts it with **But**? How would it be different if the sentence were joined on to sentence 3?

Active writing

Writers sometimes use language in unexpected ways for effect. This makes it difficult for students who have been taught 'never begin a sentence with *and* or *but*' and 'sentences always contain verbs'.

Nigel Slater – like a lot of successful writers – breaks those rules. Using two columns . . .

◆ write a paragraph saying why writers shouldn't break the rules
◆ write another paragraph saying why it *is* sometimes acceptable.

HOW TO ...
use full stops, question marks and exclamation marks

Exploring language

Activity 1

Read these sentences. In each one the normal punctuation marks have been replaced by strange symbols.

At each symbol, decide:
◆ which punctuation mark is needed (. , " ? !)
◆ whether you need to change any letters to capitals.

Thank you for your letter✳ I was really pleased to hear from you ❢ although it was also a bit of a surprise after all this time✜ when I told Tom that you'd been in touch❖ he said⊙ really◆ I can't believe it⌂❀✳ he sends his best wishes✻ as do the rest of the family✳

Use this grid to decide which punctuation marks should replace each symbol:

		Which punctuation mark would you add?	Capital letter needed – yes/no?
1	✳		
2	❢		
3	✜		
4	❖		
5	⊙		
6	◆		
7	⌂		
8	❀		
9	✻		
10	✳		

Activity 2

a Which were the easiest symbols to replace with punctuation marks?
b Which were the most difficult to replace?
c Which symbols could really be replaced by only one type of punctuation mark?
d Which could be replaced by more than one type?

Activity 3 Decide which punctuation marks you would use at the ends of these sentences:

    a You're not going in there✳
    b Watch out✳
    c So you like the soup✳
    d What time do you expect to arrive✳

Activity 4 Compare the punctuation marks you have chosen in Activity 3 with those chosen by others in the group.

    a Are there any sentences which could end in different punctuation marks?
    b What was the main clue you used to decide whether to use a full stop, exclamation mark or question mark?

Activity 5 Think of one sentence which could end with either a full stop, a question mark or an exclamation mark.

Here's an example:

The train's already arrived.
The train's already arrived?
The train's already arrived!

Activity 6 Read the sentences in Activity 5 aloud and listen to how you speak each sentence differently. How do you use your voice to show the sentence function (statement, question, exclamation)?

Activity 7 Try to describe the rules for how you move your voice for each sentence type, like this:

(punctuation mark) makes your voice go down at the end of the sentence.
(punctuation mark) makes your voice go up at the end of the sentence.
(punctuation mark) makes you say the sentence a bit more loudly, or faster, or more urgently.

Activity 8  Write a ten-line sketch about two people trapped in a lift, in which they use these sentence functions:

Statement
Question
Command
Exclamation

Label the sentence function for each line. You might use this as your starting-point:

A:	We're stuck.	*Statement*
B:	You think so?	*Question*
A:	Of course I think so!	*Exclamation*
B:	Stop shouting.	*Command*
A:	Why should I?	*Question*

Core knowledge

Punctuation helps us to communicate our meaning in writing. Punctuation marks can:
◆ show sentence boundaries, where one idea ends and another begins
◆ show other information – for example, the function of a sentence (whether it is a statement, question, command or exclamation).

There is usually little choice about punctuation marks to use at sentence boundaries:
◆ full stops to mark the end of sentences
◆ exclamation marks to mark the end of an exclamation, to add emphasis and impact in a forceful sentence
◆ question marks to mark the end of a question, drawing the reader into a text.

Other punctuation marks – such as commas, dashes, semi-colons, and colons – are used *within* sentences. They help make meanings clearer, but can also be more a matter of personal style. There is more about these punctuation marks in later units.

Practising the skill

Activity 9

The text below has no punctuation. As a result it is very difficult to follow. Use full stops, question marks and exclamation marks to show sentence boundaries.

Download this resource from the Active Grammar website

Hyenas

People don't like hyenas why should this be they are very unpopular creatures this is because their low hind-quarters, crooked legs and brutal faces can make them seem ugly they also have an offensive smell their habits are fairly disgusting

What do we know about their eating habits enough to feel ill they like to eat dung, refuse and sometimes baby hyenas they kill their prey by tearing out their intestines because they eat very quickly a pack of fifteen animals can eat a 400 lb wildebeest in four hours leaving only the bones and teeth.

Activity 10

- ◆ Were all of the sentence boundaries in this paragraph easy to spot?
- ◆ Which (if any) were the difficult ones?
- ◆ Why?

Active writing

A

Write two paragraphs without using punctuation between sentences. Choose from the topics below. In one paragraph, try to use mostly short, simple sentences. In the other try to use mostly compound and complex sentences. In both paragraphs, try to use some:

◆ statements
◆ questions
◆ commands.

But remember to leave out all the punctuation.

Topic A: simple sentences
◆ A description of the room you are in.
◆ Instructions for using a computer program
◆ The opening of a story about a car breaking down in the middle of nowhere . . . at night

Topic B: compound and complex sentences
◆ A child's description of his or her first day at school
◆ A paragraph from a letter complaining about food in a service station
◆ The opening of a speech about school uniform

B

Give your two paragraphs to someone else, and look at another person's paragraphs. Using red ink, mark on the punctuation you would use between sentences. Give feedback on:

a which sentence boundaries were hardest to spot – those in paragraph A or B
b whether there were any points when they could have used more than one punctuation mark.

C

Write down five hints to younger students on how to know when to use full stops, exclamation and question marks.

HOW TO ...
use the comma effectively as a boundary signpost in sentences

Exploring language

Activity 1 In which of these sentences would you add a comma?

1 After the rain had fallen we noticed the rainbow appear.

2 Although it was starting to get sunny the morning air still felt cold.

3 My mum who had felt ill that morning went out for a walk.

4 First she put on her old battered raincoat.

5 The coat which was covered in specks of dust looked old and messy.

6 She looked different really different

7 She said 'What are you looking at me like that for?'

8 She looked at me and seemed a bit upset and I said nothing

9 I wondered what she was thinking looked at her closely and waited for her to ask me what I thought about the coat.

10 I lied telling her how nice it looked.

Activity 2 Group sentences 1–10 into three categories:

A	B	C
Sentences where a comma is *essential*	Sentences where a comma is *helpful*	Sentences where a comma is *unnecessary*

Activity 3  For the sentences in box A, make a list of reasons that the comma was essential in those sentences.

You might set it out like this:

In the box A sentences, commas were essential because they . . .
*
*
*

Write a list of reasons for box B and box C also.

Activity 4 Based on these reasons for using commas, think of an advice sheet on placing commas in sentences. Set it out as five hints on a piece of paper.

Activity 5 Based on your discussions about using commas, write down a final hint:

Times when you should avoid using commas.

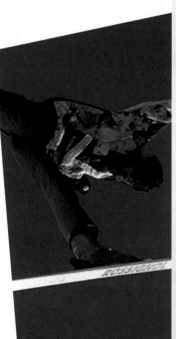

Core knowledge

Commas are used *within* sentences to help clarify meanings for the reader. Sometimes commas are essential for the reader to understand the meaning of a sentence. Sometimes the commas may not be essential, but they do clarify the ideas.

Commas are used:

◆ to separate items in a list or strings of adjectives, e.g. The cold, dark night was approaching;
◆ to introduce direct speech and replace the full stop at the end of the spoken sentence, e.g. He said, 'Hello.' 'Hi,' she replied;
◆ to mark off a relative clause, e.g. The car, which was now repaired, moved off along the street;
◆ to mark off many connecting adverbs, e.g. Quickly, she hid herself;
◆ to attach a question tag to a statement, e.g. You do understand this, don't you?;
◆ after a subordinate clause which begins a sentence, e.g. Because the weather had changed, we went indoors.

One area of writing that can lose you marks in an exam is when the comma is used instead of a full stop *between* sentences. This is known as the **comma splice**, and falling into this trap can prevent you from getting the highest grades in English.

The next part of this unit will help you to avoid the comma splice.

Practising the skill

Activity 6  For each of the sample pieces below, write down how many commas there should be, if any.

1 Melt the chocolate put it in the pan turn the heat down so that the chocolate warms through gently

2 The wind was blowing the rain was falling I walked home

3 I put the computer away it felt heavy like a slab of stone

4 The car which was dark blue roared off at speed I followed it

5 My uncle has arrived he looked older

Activity 7 Chris, in Year 8, has problems with the comma splice, as this extract from one of his assignments shows. Put yourself in the role of Punctuation Doctor and see what advice you would give.

A worrying lesson

During the next lesson he asked if he could go to the computer room. He was allowed. He stood up, his heart was pounding, he walked into the room. It was quiet. He noticed someone near the printer, he sat down at a computer and started typing. The person near the printer got up and moved towards him. He didn't know who it was, he hadn't seen him before.

Write your doctor's diagnosis. What is going on in Chris's work? What do you notice about *when* he uses comma splices? Use this template to write your notes:

The Punctuation Doctor Walton-on-the-Hill
'Colons inspected. Participles undangled.'

Chris shows some tendencies to use the comma splice. He uses full stops quite accurately most of the time, and then a sudden rash of commas appears between sentences instead of within them.

I have examined his sample and noticed the comma splice between these sentences . . .:

Looking at when he uses commas instead of full stops, there does seem to be a pattern. He uses commas when . . .

As a cure, I prescribe . . .

Signed

Activity 8 In this paragraph the punctuation has been left out. Sometimes you will need to add a full stop and sometimes a comma. Decide where you would use full stops and commas, and give a reason (e.g. a full stop to mark the boundary between two sentences). Possible reasons are given below.

Dr Miller looked worried in fact she looked very worried she picked up the large brown folder from her desk noticing as she did so the layer of dust that was gathering there and she sat back to read the notes they suggested problems serious problems Dr Miller reached forward to the telephone and pressed the small red button on its side her secretary's voice came through 'Yes Doctor' said the voice 'Phone the hospital please Angela' said Dr Miller a note of concern in her voice 'I think I need a second opinion on this' she put the phone down spun her seat round to her bookcase and lifted out a large leather-bound book it was called 'Diseases and Superstitions' Dr Miller laid it on her desk and started with absolute concentration to flick through it she stopped at the letter 'W' 'Now then' she murmured 'What has this got to say about werewolves?'

Possible reasons

Comma	Full stop
a to separate items in a list, e.g. The cold, dark night was approaching;	**g** to mark the end of a sentence
b to introduce direct speech and replace the full stop at the end of the spoken sentence;	**h** occasionally to show an abbreviation that ends with the same letter as the shortened word (e.g. Mr., Dr.)
c to mark off a relative clause, e.g. The car, which was now repaired, moved off along the street;	
d to mark off many connecting adverbs, e.g. Quickly, she hid herself;	
e to attach a question tag to a statement, e.g. You do understand this, don't you?;	
f after a subordinate clause which begins a sentence, e.g. Because the weather had changed, we went indoors.	

Active writing

A

Write a paragraph which demonstrates each of the different uses of commas. Write it on sugar paper, large enough to be displayed. Then label the different uses of the commas to explain to other classes how commas can be used.

B

Read this comment:

'In some sentences I'm not sure whether to use commas or full stops. Is there an easy way to remember?'

Write down three hints on how to know whether to use commas or full stops.

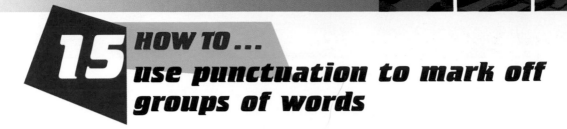

15 HOW TO...
use punctuation to mark off groups of words

Exploring language

Activity 1 Read this information text about crocodiles. It is packed with details. Why is it so difficult to follow the author's meaning?

Crocodiles amphibious carnivorous reptiles fill humans with terror. They are the perfect killing machines for example able to hold their breath under water for long periods up to an hour and with jaws capable of closing with huge force up to 13 tons. Their external organs i.e. their nostrils and ears are watertight when they submerge and their distinctive colouring greens, browns and yellows makes them almost invisible. Although we humans fear them, we also hunt them and their skins used for handbags and furniture can prove extremely valuable around £1.50 per belly inch. Inside the stomachs of crocodiles not a pretty sight large stones have been found sometimes weighing up to 30 lb. It is thought that these have been swallowed to help grind up their food such as hippo bones which would otherwise take a long period to digest but it may be that the stones are swallowed deliberately in order to help the creatures stay beneath the water more easily leaving just their nostrils above the surface.

Activity 2 What advice would you give to the writer about how to make the text clearer for a reader to follow?
Think of three hints.

Activity 3 Some punctuation marks work well in pairs:

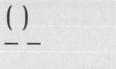

( )

– –

, ,

Take this sentence from the text and use the punctuation marks above to help clarify the meaning.

Their external organs i.e. their nostrils and ears are watertight when they submerge and their distinctive colouring greens, browns and yellows makes them almost invisible.

Core knowledge

Some punctuation is used in pairs to mark off bits of information. This can help the reader to make sense of a writer's meaning.

◆ Use **dashes** to isolate – or add – an extra point within a sentence. They can emphasize a point that is important, e.g.
They looked at the man – his name was Robert – and smiled.

◆ Use **brackets** to mark off words which are not part of the main sentence. This can be especially useful for background information, e.g.
Using chemicals to try to change everyday metals into gold (alchemy is the official term) has been around for centuries.

◆ Use **parenthetical commas** to clarify the meaning of a text without drawing too much attention to the smaller unit of meaning, e.g.
Robert, who was late getting up that morning, ran for the train.

Crocodiles, worshipped by the ancient Egyptians, are now mostly feared by humans.

Practising the skill

Activity 4   Take the whole crocodile text (Activity 1) and make it more interesting. Use brackets, dashes and commas to mark off smaller units of meaning. Then, using a highlighter and a red pen, label your rewritten text to show why you have used each type of punctuation mark. These labels should help a reader to understand how you reached your decision.

Active writing

Design a self-help leaflet on the punctuation used to mark off units of meaning. Your leaflet should:

◆ Explain what brackets, dashes and parenthetical commas can do
◆ Provide some examples of your own
◆ Give examples from texts you have researched, labelled to show how the writer is using the punctuation marks.

16 HOW TO ...
use speech punctuation accurately

Exploring language

Activity 1 Read this paragraph and see if you can work out who is speaking to whom.

Tom walked into the classroom and said hello how are you I said fine he replied that's good he said so what lesson have you got next Geography yes Geography I replied it's my favourite lesson after English said Tom.

Activity 2 One way of sorting the text out is by adding full stops. In pairs, decide where full stops should be added to the text.

Activity 3 The text won't become really clear until you use speech punctuation. That will help you to show who is saying what.

Again working in pairs, write two versions of the text – one each. Aim to create two completely different versions of the text, using these openings to get you started:

Version 1

Tom walked into the classroom and said 'Hello, how are you?' I said, 'Fine.' . . .

Version 2

Tom walked into the classroom and said, 'Hello.' 'How are you?' I said . . .

Activity 4 Does it make any difference where you put the speech verb in dialogue? This is the He said part of a sentence. For example, is there any difference in the way these sentences work?

Speech verb **before** the words spoken:
Tom walked into the classroom and **said**, 'Hello, how are you?'

Speech verb **after** the words spoken:
Tom walked into the classroom. 'Hello, how are you?' he **said**.

Speech verb **between** the words spoken:
Tom walked into the classroom. 'Hello,' he **said**. 'How are you?'

Activity 5 Take the story construction kit below and create a short extract of dialogue. Try to place the speech verbs in different places throughout your text – some before, some during, and some after what is spoken.

Download this resource from the Active Grammar website

Story construction kit – choose one option and use the setting and dialogue to construct a story.

		Dialogue	
Option	Setting	Character 1:	Character 2:
A	Outside a hospital	Name: Kerrie Hi. Are you just on your way in to see Tina? Yes, I've just seen her and she seems fine. She's pretty shaken up though about how the accident happened. Got to dash. See you.	Name: Sian Hi. Yes, I've got her some chocolates. Have you already been to visit? How is she? See you later.
B	Headteacher's office	Name: Dr Sanders Come in. Ah Sam. Sit down. Now what was it you wanted to talk to me about? I see. Fine. You realize this is a fairly serious complaint you're making?	Name: Sam Cayford Thank you. I wanted to make a complaint about the food served in the school canteen. I think it's really poor quality and encourages students to get into bad eating habits. Yes, but I think it's really important.

Activity 6

Explore some ways of avoiding direct speech. Reported speech takes away the speech marks, like this:

'You're very lucky,' said the doctor.
Becomes
The doctor said that she was very lucky *or*
The doctor told her that she was very lucky.

Take this passage of direct speech and convert it into reported speech.

The man said, 'I need some money urgently.'
'I haven't got any cash,' she replied.
'But without some money I can't get home,' he said.
She said, 'I'm sorry but I can't help.'
The man said, 'I'm going to report you to your supervisor.'

Activity 7

Now compare the reported speech with the direct speech passage. How does the text feel different?

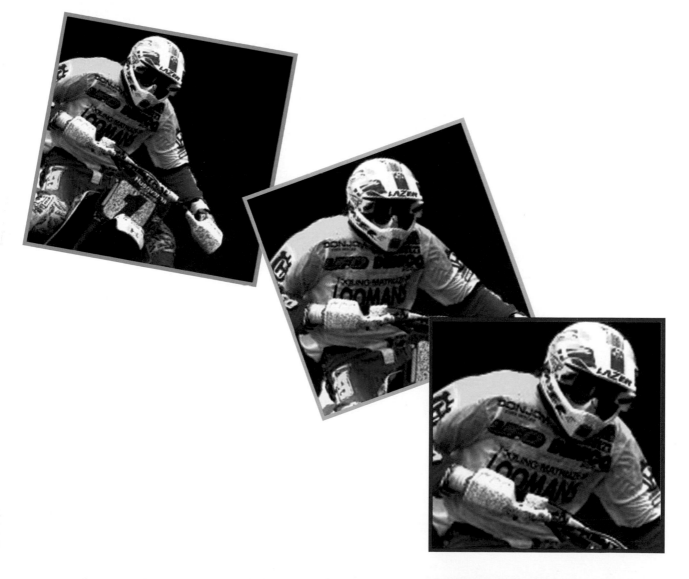

Core knowledge

- In **direct speech**, the words a person says are placed inside speech marks.
- The speech verb (he **said**, she **replied**, he **whispered**, she **yelled**) can be placed before, during or after the spoken words.
- A comma is usually used to lead into or out of the spoken words:

> Ken said, 'It's good to see you.'
> 'Thank you,' said Barbie.

- **Reported speech** is useful for creating variety in a text. It can tell us what a character said without interrupting the flow of the narrative – like this:

> Ken said that he was pleased to see Barbie. She thanked him.

Here are the essential rules of direct speech. The example below gives you more hints on making speech clear.

1 Use speech marks around the words a person actually says.
2 Place each new speaker's words on a different line, as if you were beginning a new paragraph.
3 Start the spoken words with a capital letter.
4 Always place a punctuation mark at the end of the speech marks, on the inside. This might be a full stop, question mark, exclamation mark or comma.

Example

Capital letter at the start of the speaker's words

New speaker, new line.

'I feel sick,' said my brother.

I replied, 'You're kidding.' *Punctuation marks at the end of the words – on the inside*

'Afraid not,' he said.

'Well,' I said, 'that'll teach you to watch daytime TV.'

Comma shows that the sentence continues.

If the speaker's words fall into two sections, the second section does not need a capital letter.

Practising the skill

Activity 8 Create a section of dialogue from a short story. Two people – Sean and Charlotte – think they may have just witnessed a theft at the local off-licence. They think they saw someone grab a bottle of vodka and walk out without paying. Now they are discussing whether to tell the shopkeeper or phone the police.

Write the passage, using dialogue.

In your text you should aim to include:

◆ Direct speech
◆ Reported speech
◆ Speech verbs placed before, during and after the dialogue.

Aim to write about 20 lines of text.

Activity 9 Draw labels to the key features of your dialogue, to show the reader where you have used the features listed in Activity 8.

Read someone else's version of the story. Discuss where they have placed the speech verbs and whether they have used reported speech at the same points as you did.

Active writing

A

Some writers tend to place the speech verb *before* what is said. Others usually place it *after* what is said.

Before:
He paused, and then said slowly in a deep voice: 'This is the Master-ring, the One Ring to rule them all.' (J.R.R. Tolkien).

After:
'And you is not my sister?' said Heaven Eyes. (David Almond)

Look at the novel you are currently working on in class. Explore a collection of short stories. Make a list of writers who seem mostly to place the speech verb before, those who place it after, and those who vary the position of the speech verb.

writing

B

Discuss what difference the position of the speech verb makes. Choose an extract of dialogue from a story, and see how it sounds if you move the speech verb to a different position. For example:

'And you is not my sister?' said Heaven Eyes.
becomes
Heaven Eyes said, 'And you is not my sister?'

How do they feel different? Are there any rules here? Finish these two statements:

◆ Placing the speech verb **before** the words spoken has this effect . . .
◆ Placing the speech verb **after** the words spoken has this effect . . .

17 HOW TO...
use colons and semi-colons

Exploring language

Activity 1 Look at the sentences below. Is there any other punctuation mark (e.g. full stop, comma, dash) you could put instead of the colon?

I still need the following advice: how to change the computer's clock; how to clear the memory; how to tidy the desktop.

1 What does the colon tell you as a reader?
2 What do the semi-colons do in this sentence?

Activity 2 Now look at this list. Why do you think the writer uses commas rather than semi-colons?

You need to get the following: cheese, two large potatoes, six medium eggs, some milk.

Activity 3 Here's another list. Why do you think the writer uses semi-colons, rather than commas?

You need to get the following: a large piece of half-fat cheddar cheese; two large potatoes for baking, preferably ready-washed; six medium free-range eggs; some semi-skimmed milk.

Activity 4 Generate some rules:

When writing lists, colons are useful because they . . .
When writing lists, semi-colons are useful for . . .

Activity 5 Read this compound sentence:

Rick wants to go to America and Hayley wants to go to Australia.

Now look what happens if you use a semi-colon to replace the conjunction and:

Rick wants to go to America; Hayley wants to go to Australia.

Because these two sentences are about the same topic (where to go), the semi-colon can join them together.

In which of these sentences could you use a semi-colon to replace the conjunction?

1 Pete likes fish and Trevor likes chicken.
2 The boat smashed against the dock and it began to rain.
3 My hand was feeling numb but it was too late to see a doctor.
4 The skate-park was empty and a few birds swirled above it.

◆ Write down the examples where you can use a semi-colon instead of the conjunction.
◆ How does this change the feel of the sentence?
◆ If you can't use a semi-colon in any of sentences 1–4, try to say why not.

Core knowledge

Sometimes in writing, a full stop feels too 'strong' to separate two sentences. Colons and semi-colons can help.

◆ **Colons** are like car headlights: they point to things in front. This can be really useful at the start of lists and to introduce a quotation. Examples:
for **introducing a list:** These are the things we will need: two hammers, a spade and a set of screwdrivers.
for **introducing a quotation:** Feste's song is haunting and sad: "When that I was an a little tiny boy..."
for **introducing a statement:** One thing is certain: Malvolio has learnt his lesson.

◆ **Semi-colons** separate longer items in a list, to make it clearer for the reader. Example:
These are the things we will need: two brand-new hammers; a garden spade or hoe (whichever you have available); a set of screwdrivers

◆ They can also link two sentences about the same topic, or make two clear points
(same topic): The street was empty; it seemed calm.
(two points): The first half of the match was lively; the second half was pretty boring.

Practising the skill

Activity 6 Look at this information text about pigeons. Where the numbered symbols are, decide which punctuation mark you would use – colon, semi-colon or full stop. Then, using the list below, give a reason for your choice (e.g. 2B or 3A).

1 Full stop	2 Colon	3 Semi-colon
A To show the end of a unit of meaning	**A** To introduce a list	**A** To join two linked items in a sentence
	B To introduce a quotation or statement	**B** To separate two topics within a sentence

Download this resource from the Active Grammar website

Homing-pigeons **1** plump, small-billed birds **2** homing-pigeons still amaze us **3** we are still not sure how they find their way home **4** some people used to believe that they used landmarks along the route to know which way to go **5** other people believe they use the sun to navigate **6** one thing is certain **7** they have an amazing skill which can be very useful to humans **8** the most famous example of the homing-pigeon's talents dates back to 1845 **9** this bird belonged to the Duke of Wellington **10** one of his pigeons dropped dead a mile from its home in London **11** it had been released 55 days earlier in the West Indies **12** in that time it had travelled 5,400 miles **13** no wonder it was exhausted **14**

Activity 7 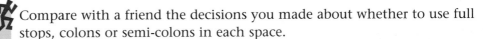 Compare with a friend the decisions you made about whether to use full stops, colons or semi-colons in each space.

Which places were the easiest and hardest for you to decide on the punctuation mark? Why?

Active writing

Design a poster or leaflet, for display in your classroom, which shows other students how colons and semi-colons can be useful in their work. Give examples of how they might be used in literature essays and in instructions.

Use a combination of hints (try using a colon to introduce a quotation ...), instructions (use semi-colons when you need to separate longer items in a list) and examples.

HOW TO...
give pace, variety and emphasis to your writing

Exploring language

Activity 1 Read through this paragraph by Vicky. She says:

'I wrote it quickly and when I read it back it seemed pretty boring. I can see now that I've joined all my ideas together with <u>and</u>, <u>but</u> or <u>or</u>.'

> The girl was in the house and it was dark but she didn't mind and she was watching TV but then she thought she heard a sound upstairs. She thought it was probably just a window flapping open or a floorboard creaking but then she heard it again and she started to worry a bit more. She opened the lounge door and decided to go upstairs and put on the light.

Advice to Vicky:

You have written this text using compound sentences. That means your sentences tend to be joined by and and but. To add more variety to your written style you could try:

◆ starting with a past participle (-ed), e.g. Worri**ed**, the girl switched on the lights
◆ starting with a present participle (-ing), e.g. Hurry**ing**, she made her way out of the room
◆ starting with a connective, e.g. **Although** she was nervous, she headed upstairs
◆ putting the subject halfway through a sentence instead of at the beginning, e.g. At the top of the stairs, the creature waited.

Experiment with rewriting Vicky's paragraph, using the suggestions above.

Activity 2  Read these three texts aloud. All are on the subject of gorillas.
- ◆ Which is most interesting?
- ◆ Which is most boring?

Text A
Gorillas love their food. Their food tastes bitter to humans. They like leaves, fruit and nuts. They do not eat meat. They do not drink much. They get moisture from their food. Gorillas are usually fat. They live in tropical forests. In the past they lived in mountain forests. They have wide nostrils. These help them to breathe thin air at high altitudes.

Text B
Much of the food eaten by gorillas tastes bitter to humans. Whilst they like leaves, fruit and nuts, they very rarely eat meat. Nor do they drink much. Instead they obtain moisture from their food. Gorillas are usually fat. Although they are now found chiefly in tropical forests, gorillas once lived in mountain forests where their wide nostrils helped them to breathe the thin air at high altitudes.

Text C
Gorillas eat mostly leaves, fruit and nuts and very rarely eat meat and much of the food they eat tastes bitter to humans but, unlike us, they do not drink much. They get their moisture from the food and are usually fat. They live in tropical forests but used to live in mountain forests and they have wide nostrils and this helped them to breathe air at high altitudes.

Activity 3  Brainstorm some of the ways in which the writer has tried to vary the sentence style.

Core knowledge

Successful writing is interesting for a number of reasons. Of course the content is important – what you write about. The words you choose are also vital. But it's important to remember that using a range of sentence structures makes a big difference. It helps hold the reader's interest.

Good writing usually has a *variety* of sentences, as well as interesting, well-chosen vocabulary. Varying your sentences can be done in a number of ways:

Sentence variety hints

Simple sentences:

1 Try a very short sentence – e.g.
They don't.   Gorillas are fat.

2 Try a simple sentence with more modification to carry detail – e.g.
They simply don't.   Gorillas are generally fat.

Compound sentences:

3 Use the connectives and, but or or to combine simple sentences.
Make a sentence with two clauses or more.
Experiment with how long a compound sentence can become before it feels uncontrolled.

Complex sentences:

4 Use a relative clause to modify a simple sentence – e.g.
Gorillas eat fruit and nuts. They rarely eat meat.
⇩
could become
⇩
Gorillas, which eat fruit and nuts, rarely eat meat.
or
Gorillas, which rarely eat meat, mostly eat fruit and nuts.

5 Use a present participle (*-ing* verb) to create two-part sentence – e.g.
Living in the tropical forests, they mostly eat leaves, fruit and nuts.

6 Use an adverbial clause to create two-part sentences, like this:
Although they now live in tropical forests, they used to live on mountains.
or
Because they live in tropical forests, they mostly eat leaves, fruit and nuts.
or
They mostly eat leaves, fruit and nuts **because they live in tropical forests**.

Adverbial clauses begin with words like:
Although   Despite   Because   Whenever   After

and phrases like:
In spite of   Even though

Practising the skill

Activity 4

Write the most boring paragraph you can on one of the topics below. Make it boring by using unexciting vocabulary and a very small range of sentences (e.g. use simple sentences all the time, or keep joining clauses using *and* or *but* or *or*).

Boring topics:

Why I like cheese
My journey to school
The view from the window in this classroom

Aim to write six to ten sentences.

Activity 5

Read the boring paragraph written by a friend.

Give it a 'boring' rating:

1 = not boring enough
3 = fairly boring
5 = deeply boring.

Activity 6

Now take on the role of 'Boring Consultant' and cure your friend's boring writing. Take what he or she has written and make it more interesting by giving the sentences more variety. Use these ideas:

◆ start with an '-ed' word
◆ start with an '-ing' word
◆ start with a connective (e.g. **despite**, **although**)
◆ put the subject halfway through a sentence (*moseying down the street, **the cowboy** felt nervous*)

Then talk your friend through what you have done to 'cure' the writing.

Active writing

A

Here is a boring paragraph. It takes a not-very-exciting topic and then, using simple sentences, keeps it not very exciting.

See how far you can inject some interest by rewriting it using a variety of sentences – simple, compound and complex. Keep referring back to the six possibilities in the core knowledge panel in order to create these different types of sentence. Experiment with as many sentence styles as you can.

Margarine

Margarine was invented in 1860. It started with a competition. The French Government was worried about butter shortages. They looked for something different. They held a contest. Mege Mouries won. He heated beef fat. Then he added pigs' gastric juices. Then he added water. He skimmed the substance. He added milk. He churned the substance. He kneaded the solids. This was the first margarine.

B

Compare your version of the paragraph about margarine with a friend's. Listen to the way other people in your group have rewritten the paragraph. Vote on which shows most variety.

19 ACTIVE READING
Exploring sentence variety in instructional writing

You might expect instructional writing, such as recipe books, to use commands all the time. As this extract from Delia Smith shows, instructional writing can use a variety of sentence types and sentence functions.

❶ Find an example of a statement.

❷ Find an example of a question.

❸ Find an example of a command or instruction.

How to tell how old a raw egg is while it is safely tucked away in its shell could seem a bit tricky, but not so. Remember the air pocket? There is a simple test that tells you exactly how much air there is. All you do is place the egg in a tumbler of cold water: if it sinks to a completely horizontal position, it is very fresh; if it tilts up slightly or to a semi-horizontal position, it could be up to a week old; if it floats into a vertical position, then it is stale.

Delia Smith,
How to Cook Book 1,
BBC Books

❹ How does Delia Smith make the process sound simple and straightforward?

❺ Why do you think she uses a question in sentence 2?

❻ What impression do you get of Delia Smith's relationship with her audience?

Active writing

◆ Rewrite the text as a set of instructions in a more impersonal style. You might use bullet-points or numbers to list the instructions.

◆ Write a paragraph saying how the text feels different if rewritten in this way.

20 HOW TO...
vary the rhythm of sentences

Exploring language

Activity 1   Here are the openings of three mystery stories. Read the three paragraphs aloud. Which one is *most* successful in building suspense? Which one is *least* successful?

1   The air was cold and it was getting dark but still the bus hadn't arrived. I was waiting at the edge of the town where I always waited for the evening bus home. I looked at my watch and thought to myself: 'It's usually here by now.'

2   Cold air swirled around my body and I pulled my coat tighter. Looking towards the darkening sky I thought I could sense rain. I glanced at my watch and saw that it was way past the time when the bus usually arrived. Worried but helpless, I could only wait.

3   The air was bitter. A bad night was brewing. I shuffled my feet, trying to keep warm, and looked at the sky. Rain. No doubt about it. I pulled my coat tighter. I looked at my watch. There was nothing I could do but watch and wait.

See if you agree with a friend about which text is best at building suspense.

Activity 2   How does your chosen text create suspense? Is it the **vocabulary** or the **sentence patterns**?

You can test for this by blanking out the **lexical** words. These are the words that carry the main *information* in a text. This will leave you with just the **grammatical** words – the words that provide the *structure*.

For example:
The air was cold

Lexical words = air; cold
Grammatical words = the; was

Blank out the lexical words and the sentence looks like this:
The *** was ***.

GLOSSARY

Lexical and grammatical words

Lexical words carry the specific message in our sentences. When children use telegrammatic language (between saying their first word and speaking in full sentences), they mostly use lexical words:

Car go fast

Grammatical words are the words that give structure in sentences:

The ____ is ___ ____

For more about telegrammatic language, see page 11.

1 In one extract, choose the lexical words to blank out.

2 Replace them with ***.

3 Now read the passage out again. When you come to a blanked out lexical word (***) say blah. At first it will just sound silly. Read it aloud until people are able to concentrate on the rhythm of each sentence, rather than the content.

> **Remember:**
> **Lexical words** are those that carry information in a text.
> **Grammatical words** are those that provide structure.
> For example, in Text 1 the lexical words/phrases include: air; cold; getting dark; bus; arrived.
> The grammatical words/phrases include: The; was; and it was; but still the; hadn't.

Core knowledge

Sometimes writing can be completely accurate, but lifeless and dull to read. Choosing more interesting vocabulary is one way to liven up your work. But even with lively vocabulary a text can feel flat. This has to do with sentence variety. Different types of sentences can help you to create different rhythms in your writing, which in turn help to hold the reader's interest.

Practising the skill

Activity 3

Short, simple sentences are useful for building tension. Read aloud the paragraphs below. Some repeat the same sentence structure; others have more variety.

◆ Which do you think is the *most* varied piece of writing?
◆ Which has *least* variety of sentence types?

All the paragraphs are about computers. For best effect, read them aloud.

Sample A

My printer isn't working. It is frustrating. The paper is jammed. I am cross. I have called the engineer. It will be a long wait. The engineer is busy.

Comment:
Variety (none) 1 2 3 4 5 (lots)

Sample B

My printer isn't working and I'm annoyed because I've got lots of stuff to print out. There's nothing I can do and I've decided to phone the engineer. I'll see if she can sort out the problem.

Comment:
Variety (none) 1 2 3 4 5 (lots)

Sample C

My printer isn't working. It's driving me mad because I've got lots of stuff to print out. There's nothing I can do about it. I've decided to phone the engineer to see if she can sort out the problem.

Comment:
Variety (none) 1 2 3 4 5 (lots)

Active writing

Hold a class reading of opening paragraphs of different texts. Read them aloud and listen to the way the writer uses rhythm and sentence variety.

Use a range of texts – from newspapers, instructions, stories, cookery books, and so on.

◆ Which texts have the most interesting rhythm of sentences?
◆ How much difference is there between fiction and non-fiction texts?

Make a display of opening paragraphs. Write your comments on the use of sentences in each paragraph and place these comments with the texts.

21 HOW TO ...
develop the right sentence style for formal written work

Exploring language

Activity 1 Read these six sentences. Each expresses an apology. Place them in order of *least* formal (1) to *most* formal (6) by placing the letter against a number . . .

a I regret that I shall be unable to attend.
b Sorry – can't make it.
c I'm afraid I won't be able to be there.
d I will not be able to attend.
e Apologies – I'm otherwise engaged.
f I'm doing other things that night.

Activity 2 **Formal to informal**

Look at these two formal sentences. What would you change to make them informal? Write down an informal version, and make a note of your key changes.

a Formal version: Her arrival at school today will be delayed

b Formal version: Would you be so good as to pass the sugar, please?

Informal to formal

Look at these two informal sentences. What would you change to make them formal? Write down a formal version, and make a note of your key changes.

c Informal version: You're dead right about that.

d Informal version: I was just phoning to check you're okay.

Activity 3 Based on the activities above, brainstorm two main differences between *formal* and *informal* expression. Use these statements as starting-points:

The vocabulary in informal sentences is often _____ –
for example:
The verb forms in informal sentences are often _____ –
for example:

Activity 4 In which of these contexts would you use formal (F) or informal (I) language?

a Writing a postcard to a best friend.
b Writing a literature assignment.
c Writing to complain about a 40-minute delay in a bus journey.
d Speaking to an important school visitor.
e Speaking to your tutor about your progress this year.
f Speaking to a friend about a CD you bought at the weekend.

Activity 5 Now put the six contexts (a–f) in order of *most* to *least* formal. Look at your list. Does writing always tend to be more formal than speaking?

Core knowledge

When . . .?

Formal language is often used:

◆ when we are talking or writing to people we don't know well
◆ when addressing a group
◆ on a formal topic (e.g. talking about a heart operation is likely to be more formal than talking about the posters in your bedroom).

Informal language is often used

◆ when we are talking or writing to people we know well
◆ when the topic is something familiar (e.g. a favourite TV programme, rather than the history of World War I).

How . . .?

Formal language uses more complex words. These may be:

Longer words with more syllables (a+pol+o+gies rather than sor+ry)
Technical or old words (abode rather than house)
Formal language uses expanded verb structures (will not rather than won't).

Practising the skill

Activity 6

Students Hamid and David have been asked to write literature assignments comparing two poems. Their teacher has stressed the need for a formal style. Read their first paragraphs.

◆ Which style seems more appropriate?
◆ What advice would you give to each student about changing the style?

Hamid

In his poem Seamus Heaney depicts a childhood world. He regrets its demise and remains nostalgic for the days when picking blackberries was a significant moment in his life. He recalls in vivid detail the 'dark-eyed berries'.

David

Seamus Heaney's poem is all about when he was a child. He looks back to the time when he went out picking blackberries and feels really sad about the way those days have passed. I think he probably wishes he was back in this time with the rest of his family because it seems to be a really important time for him.

Active writing

A

Which of the two samples from Hamid and David do you prefer?

Take the one you think is worse, and rewrite it in a style that is more suitable for a literature assignment.

B

Write the opening paragraph for a literature assignment of your own on a book you are reading at the moment.

22 ACTIVE READING
Exploring sentence variety in fiction

Annie Proulx writes stories set in the hard, barren landscapes of Wyoming, USA.

Use the question sequence to explore the way she uses language – in particular, active verbs.

The Governors of Wyoming

The quick thunderstorm was over, the street wet and slices of tingling blue showing through bunched cloud. They waited in the truck. Roany had parked close to the newsstand, the stop for the Denver bus. A few raindrops fell, hard as dice. At five thirty-five the bus pulled in, stinking, sighing. Eleven passengers descended, Wade Walls the last. He shot them a glance without turning his head when Roany put the window down and said his name. They watched him cross the street and go into the Ranger Bar.

Annie Proulx

❶ Look at the way Annie Proulx uses **modification**. In some places she modifies nouns with adjectives (*tingling blue*, *bunched cloud*). In other places she avoids modifying her nouns (the truck, the newsstand).
a Rewrite the first sentence stripping out all the modification. See how it works now as the opening of a story.
b Rewrite sentence 2 by adding modifying adjectives (to describe the truck) and adverbs (to describe how they waited). What is the effect?

❷ To describe what the bus does, the writer uses two *-ing* verbs: *stinking*, *sighing*.
a What if she had placed each verb in a separate simple sentence instead (*it was . . .*)? How is the effect different?
b Think of two other verbs she might have used at that point to describe what the bus does.

❸ Look at the way the writer uses a **variety of sentences**. This is the pattern of her sentences:

    complex
    simple
    simple
    simple
    complex
    simple
    complex
    compound

a Try writing the paragraph entirely in simple sentences. What is the effect?
b Try writing the paragraph as one long compound sentence (using *and*, *or* or *but*). What is the effect?

❹ To give an impression of the rain, the writer uses a **simile** (*as hard as dice*).
a Think of a different noun she might have used: *as hard as _____*.
b Think of a simile that would work to describe soft snow falling, instead of hard rain.

Active writing

Imagine the text if it were an eyewitness statement. Imagine someone is watching the scene and has been asked by the police to describe what they saw.

Think about:

◆ how the description would be different (would it be less vivid, more straightforward?)
◆ how the sentence structure might differ (more simple and compound sentences?)
◆ using a first person voice (*I saw . . . I noticed . . .*)

Write the opening section of the eyewitness statement.

23 HOW TO...
recognize and remedy ambiguity in sentences

Exploring language

Activity 1

Why are these sentences unclear and confusing?
For each sentence, write a question to highlight the problem. The first one is done for you.

The teacher talked to John about his problems.
Question: whose are the problems?

1 Jane said to Mary that she seemed happier.
2 A woman stood talking to a friend. She was about thirty.
3 Police questioned a large group of youths last night. They were very pleasant towards them.
4 The children chatted to the senior citizens. They seemed very happy.

Activity 2

Pronouns can cause problems. These include the words she, he, they, me, you, I, us, we.

Write five deliberately confusing sentences where the pronoun is unclear. Try to use five different pronouns.

Use this example to get started:

The girl sat next to the old woman. She was eating an ice cream.

Activity 3

Look at the ambiguous (confusing) sentences written by other people in your group. Say what you think they might mean.

Activity 4

Here are other examples of sentences where information could be placed in a different position to help the reader. Write down two versions of the sentence that give different meanings.

For example:
The burglar attacked the housekeeper with a bag.
could mean
The burglar used a bag to attack the housekeeper.
or
The burglar attacked the housekeeper, who had a bag.

1 The man stroked the cat with a bird in his mouth.
2 The computer engineer had problems with his client. He was sweating heavily.
3 The criminal shot at the elderly woman with a knife.
4 The doctor looked at the patient and said she was happy.
5 The crowd moved towards the gates and they fell over.
6 Alice gave the card she had made to her sister, and she was delighted with it.
7 Wanted: cooking pot for keen cook with heavy bottom.

Core knowledge

Sentences can be ambiguous. This means they can leave the reader unclear about their intended meaning. Sometimes rewriting the sentence as two separate sentences can help to make its meaning clear:

The burglar attacked the housekeeper with a bag.
The burglar had a bag. He attacked the housekeeper with it.

Sometimes punctuation can help:

The burglar, using a bag, attacked the housekeeper.

Practising the skill

Activity 5 Look at this ambiguous text. It uses so many pronouns that it is difficult to untangle what is happening. Simplify and clarify the text so that it makes more sense to the reader.

The team headed into the forest looking for animals with guns. They were only fake but they looked very realistic. Some creatures moved in the bushes. They stopped and stared. They thought they could hear breathing. They could see humans. They lifted the guns on to their shoulders with a lot of effort.

Active writing

A

Write a poster or factsheet: 'How to avoid unclear sentences'. Write five hints – with examples – on how to write clearly.

B

Copy out your group's best examples of ambiguous sentences and put them on large sheets of paper around your classroom.

24 HOW TO ...
use tense consistently, and manage shifts in tense

Exploring language

Activity 1

Look at this story opening, told in the past tense and then the present tense.

The street was quiet. Nothing moved, and Daniel felt it was probably safe to leave the bus shelter he was hiding in. He stepped out, looked about him, and set off carefully to the other side.	The street is quiet. Nothing moves, and Daniel feels it is probably safe to leave the bus shelter he is hiding in. He steps out, looks about him, and sets off carefully to the other side.

a How can you tell whether it is set in the past or present tense?
b Which are the main words in each sentence which help you to tell?
c Try to say how each version feels different.
d Which version of the story do you prefer?

Activity 2

Now look at this new version of the story. This time there are more changes of tense:

The street **had been** quiet. Nothing **had** moved, and Daniel felt it **would** probably be safe to leave the bus shelter he **had been** hiding in since lunchtime. He stepped out, looked about him, and set off carefully to the other side.

The story has been shifted further back into the past tense. Does it:

◆ become more/less dramatic?
◆ create a bigger/smaller sense of doubt about whether Daniel will be safe?

Activity 3

Choose a well-known story, such as a legend or fairy tale. Retell the first part in the present tense (is . . . are . . .)
Retell it again. This time shift it back in time (was . . . were . . .)
Retell it a third time. This time shift it further back in time again (had been . . .)

Use these examples to get you started:

◆ The three Little Pigs are doing some cleaning . . .
◆ The three Little Pigs were doing some cleaning . . .
◆ The three Little Pigs had been doing some cleaning . . .

Activity 4 Decide whether you agree with this statement:

'Stories are usually in the past tense.'
Try to think of examples which support your opinion.

Activity 5 Look at these opening sentences from information texts. Work out whether they are written in the past, present or future tense.

A

This will be an important month for you as Leo moves into your sun sign.

B

Prices are down again this month. Look at these bargains.

C

Home computers became big business when Apple ignited the market with the Macintosh.

The tense of text A is . . .
The tense of text B is . . .
The tense of text C is . . .

Activity 6 Writers can of course use different tenses within the same sentence.

Work out how examples A, B and C below combine different tenses. Compare the version of each text with the one in Activity 5 and say:

◆ what has changed
◆ how the effect is different.

A

This **will be** an important month for you as Leo **has moved** into your sun sign.

B

Prices **have been going** down again this month. **Look** at these bargains.

C

Home computers **would become** big business when Apple **ignited** the market with the Macintosh.

Core knowledge

In English, the endings of verbs are changed to show the present and past tenses:

She laugh+s … she laugh+ed

To show the future tense, we sometimes use the present tense verb with an adverbial:

The train leaves **soon**.
The train leaves **in five minutes**.
The train leaves **tomorrow**.

We can also create the future tense by using modal verbs – will/would/shall/might

The train **will** leave in five minutes.
The train **might** leave in five minutes.

Different text-types are usually (but not always) written in a particular tense:

Narrative – generally past tense, occasionally present.
Information text – generally present tense, unless about past events.
Recounts – past tense.
Explanations – present tense.
Instructions – present tense.
Persuasion – shifts tenses, depending on purpose.

Practising the skill

Activity 7 Write some instructions – e.g. for saving a document in a computer program. Use commands, with the verbs at the beginnings of your sentences, like this:

Go to 'File'. Select 'Save' . . .

Activity 8 Rewrite the instructions in Activity 7, using the modal verbs should and must, like this:

You should go to 'File'.

◆ How do the instructions seem different?
◆ Do they seem *more* or *less* friendly/direct/informative?

Activity 9  Write the opening of a text which shifts its tense, using one of the frameworks below.

Genre: autobiography	Genre: narrative
Write an opening sentence about your life now (how old you are, what you are like)	Write an opening sentence about a character set in the past – e.g. someone looking out of a window
Shift tense: write a next sentence about an early memory (e.g. what you used to be like)	Write a sentence about something that happened earlier in the day to the character (e.g. the day had started calmly, and then gone wrong)

Compare your two sentences with someone else's.

Active writing

Write the opening of a personal account, making predictions about the future. Think about what school or home might be like one day, and how they might be changed by technology.

Try to combine present, future and past tenses. Use this guide to help you shift tenses:

◆ start in the present tense: I believe/think/hope . . .
◆ continue in the future tense: it will . . .
◆ use modal verbs: we might . . .
◆ use the present tense with adverbials: in the next few years, computers are likely to . . .
◆ compare life in the past: people used to believe . . . things were once different . . .

Label your text to show the different tenses you have used.

HOW TO ...
express ideas in either the active or passive voice to suit purpose

Exploring language

Activity 1
Look at these texts written in the passive voice. Decide what type of text each one could be (e.g. a detective story, a newspaper report, a leaflet . . .)

A
A black Escort was found abandoned yesterday . . .

B
The magnesium was heated for a few seconds . . .

C
It was announced today that prices will rise . . .

Activity 2
How do the texts feel different when told in the active voice?

A
Police found a black Escort abandoned yesterday . . .

B
We heated the magnesium for a few seconds . . .

C
The Government announced today that prices will rise . . .

◆ Which sentences do you think are 'improved' by being written in the active voice?
◆ Which are better in the passive mode?

Try to say why.

Activity 3
Read these passive voice sentences. Work out what text type each one could be. Then think of a reason that the writer might want to use the passive voice. These reasons might include:

a to hide information about who did something
b because the person doing something is not really as important as what happened
c to build a sense of mystery or suspense.

Example	Where might you find this text (e.g. newspaper, textbook, novel)	Possible reason for using passive voice
1 The victim was found lying on the bedroom carpet . . .		
2 The lights were seen being switched off at 7:30		
3 I'm afraid a cup has been broken		
4 The speech was very well received		
5 People are being ripped off by some supermarkets		

Core knowledge

The passive voice turns a sentence around so that the object comes first and the subject is placed later – like this:

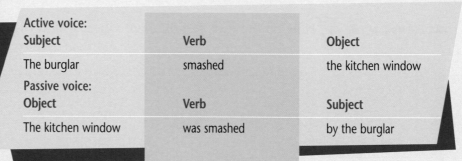

Active voice: Subject	Verb	Object
The burglar	smashed	the kitchen window
Passive voice: Object	Verb	Subject
The kitchen window	was smashed	by the burglar

The passive voice will often leave the subject out altogether:

The kitchen window was smashed.

The passive voice is not very common in most speech and writing, except in some types of texts. It can be useful where the speaker/writer wishes to:

◆ withhold information until later
◆ conceal information altogether
◆ build suspense
◆ give emphasis to what happened, rather than who did it.

Notice the difference:

a Our client did not smash the window.
b The window was not smashed by our client.

Does sentence **b** place more emphasis on the broken window and make the client seem less likely to be involved?

Practising the skill

Activity 4

Write the opening of a police report which describes *what has happened* rather than who did it. Use the example and facts below:

The back door had been left open and . . .

◆ milk spilt over the surfaces
◆ papers all over the floor
◆ a knife on the table
◆ a note saying 'back soon'

Activity 5

Imagine you live at the house described in Activity 4. You have had a bad morning and everything has gone wrong. You arrive home to find the police in your kitchen. They obviously think there has been a burglary. In fact, you have just made a mess then left the door open whilst nipping to the shops.

Take the police account you wrote in Activity 4 and rewrite it using the active voice:

I left the back door open because I was in such a rush. Earlier I had . . .

Active writing

Write some instructions for another class about how to use the active and passive voice. Demonstrate it by writing two texts, one using the active, the other using the passive voice. Place the texts side by side and use margin notes to show the key features.

You could choose from the following subjects:

◆ A police report about an abandoned car, and the account of the person who abandoned it because of heavy snow.
◆ A newspaper report about the Government's plans to give all students cheap laptop computers (active: The Government has announced . . . / passive: It was announced yesterday . . .)

26 ACTIVE READING
Exploring sentence variety in travel writing

This is the second and third paragraph of a travel book by Jonathan Raban. In it, he sets off to sail around the British Isles.

Use the question sequence to explore the way he uses language.

❶ The **first sentence** is a minor sentence – it has no verb. Rewrite it as a sentence with a verb. Use a verb like *is* or *hums* or *buzzes*. How does this change the start of the paragraph?

❷ Look at the use of **modification**, using adjectives and adverbs: *continuous slight motion . . . vaguely remember . . . bright nonsense . . . usual cruising companion . . . indignant old fool.*
Try cutting the modification so that you avoid using adjectives and adverbs. How is the text changed?

Coasting The engine, the engine. Its thump and clatter, all mixed up with the smell of diesel oil and the continuous slight motion of the sea, is so regular and monotonous that you keep on hearing voices in it. Sometimes when the revs are low, there's a man under the boards reciting poems that you vaguely remember in a resonant bass. Sometimes the noise rises to the bright nonsense of a cocktail party in the flat downstairs. At present, though, you're stuck with your usual cruising companion at sixteen hundred revs, an indignant old fool grumbling in the cellar.
Jonathan Raban

❸ Look at the use of the **pronoun** *you*. What happens if you change it to *I* and *me*? What effect does the writer create by using *you*?
❹ Look at the **sentence structure** – mostly complex. Retell the whole text in a series of short simple sentences – no details, just the facts. How many sentences does it take?
❺ Look at the **verb forms** – informal because of the elision (e.g. *you're* rather than *you are*). What happens if you expand these verb forms?
❻ The *indignant old fool* is the engine. This is a technique called **personification** – describing a machine as if it were a human being. Rewrite the text so that the engine is just an engine, not a human.

Active writing

How might the text be different if it were the start of a *short story* set on the boat?

Think about:

◆ whether you might use the first-person mode (*I* rather than *you*)
◆ the tense (will you use past rather than present?)
◆ the description (will you add more action rather than description?)

Write the opening paragraph of a short story set on this boat.

Exploring Paragraphs

Paragraphs are used to organize our writing, to help readers understand and enjoy it.

This section explores the way paragraphs are used in different types of texts, and describes ways of making sure that your ideas link together – both within and across paragraphs.

This section:

◆ builds your skills in using paragraphs
◆ teaches you about cohesion – how to link ideas together
◆ explores how sentences work *within* paragraphs
◆ describes how ideas are linked *across* paragraphs
◆ shows you how topic sentences can help signal information to readers
◆ explores different styles of paragraphing in different types of texts
◆ shows you different texts in action.

27 HOW TO ...
generate, cluster and organize ideas into paragraphs

Exploring language

Activity 1

Read these facts about washing machines.
At the moment they are jumbled up in one long paragraph.
Use letters **A** to **O** to write down what you think should be the order of the sentences.

Amazing facts about washing machines

This made the clothes tumble over each other. **A** In the 1920s the machines used electric motors underneath the hub which contained the water. **B** The first true washing machines appeared in the 1860s. **C** Washing machines did not become popular in the USA until the 1950s. **D** Motors were later added to the machines. **E** The earliest form of automatic washing machine was on sailing ships. **F** Front-loading washing machines work by bashing the clothes against the side – a bit like beating clothes on a rock. **G** Around the same time, some electric washing machines in Germany used coal-fired heating. **H** They were powered by electricity, steam, or petrol. **I** They were wooden boxes which could be turned by a handle. **J** This meant that you could sometimes get a powerful electric shock. **K** The coal was in a grate underneath the washing drum. **L** Dirty clothes would be tied to a rope and hung overboard so that they dragged through the open sea. **M** They didn't catch on until then because servant labour was still cheap and they used humans instead. **N** This was a fairly successful way of cleaning the garments. **O**

Activity 2

Group the sentences together under topic headings. You might have a heading called 'early history', another 'How washing machines work' and so on.

Decide:
a how many headings you need
b what the headings are
c which sentences should be placed under which headings.

Activity 3 Now look at how you can tell which sentences follow others.
Some are **topic sentences** – they tell you what the main topic is.
Others use pronouns (e.g. this, they, it). These tell you that they follow
topic sentences – adding information, but not introducing the main topic.
We can call these **active writing sentences**.

Example:

Topic sentence	Active writing sentence
The first true washing machines appeared in the 1860s.	They were wooden boxes which could be turned by a handle.
Q: How can you tell this is a topic sentence?	Q: How can you tell this is an active writing sentence?
A: It introduces the main subject (the first true washing machine)	A: It begins with the pronoun *They*. This shows that it must refer back to an earlier topic.

Look at sentences **a** to **g** below. Decide whether each is a topic or an active
writing sentence:

a This made the clothes tumble over each other.
b Washing machines did not become popular in the USA until the 1950s.
c Motors were later added to the machines.
d This meant that you could sometimes get a powerful electric shock.
e They were powered by electricity, steam, or petrol.
f The earliest form of automatic washing machine was on sailing ships.
g This was a fairly successful way of cleaning the garments.

GLOSSARY

Topic sentence

A sentence at the start of a text or paragraph which tells you what the content
will be. Newspaper stories usually start with topic sentences: they tell you who,
where, and when.

Example:
A 77-year-old man was dramatically rescued in York last night when flood waters
threatened to engulf his house.

Activity 4 Imagine you are writing to someone who is learning English for the first
time. Finish these two descriptions:

1 You can recognize topic sentences by . . .
2 You can recognize active writing sentences by . . .

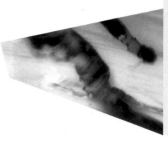

Core knowledge

Paragraphs help us to organize ideas so that the reader finds it easier to follow our meaning.

Paragraphs usually begin with topic sentences. These tell the reader what the paragraph is about.

Active writing sentences often use pronouns to refer back to the topic sentence. Pronouns include: this, they, these, that, he, she, we.

Practising the skill

Activity 5 Look again at the washing machine facts (Activity 1). This is the order in which the sentences originally appeared: F, M, O, C, J, A, E, I, B, K, H, L, D, N, G.

It has been divided into five paragraphs. See whether you agree with each paragraph break. For each dividing point (**A** to **D**), write down whether you agree or disagree. Then try to say why or why not. If you disagree, suggest a better place to break the paragraph.

Amazing facts about washing machines

The earliest form of automatic washing machine was on sailing ships. Dirty clothes would be tied to a rope and hung overboard so that they dragged through the open sea.

A

This was a fairly successful way of cleaning the garments. The first true washing machines appeared in the 1860s. They were wooden boxes which could be turned by a handle. This made the clothes tumble over each other.

B

Motors were later added to the machines. They were powered by electricity, steam, or petrol. In the 1920s the machines used electric motors underneath the hub which contained the water. This meant that you could sometimes get a powerful electric shock. Around the same time, some electric washing machines in Germany used coal-fired heating.

C

The coal was in a grate underneath the washing drum. Washing machines did not become popular in the USA until the 1950s. They didn't catch on until then because servant labour was still cheap and they used humans instead.

D
Front-loading washing machines
work by bashing the clothes against
the side – a bit like beating clothes
on a rock.

active writing

Active writing

Find three to five different texts and
look at how the writers guide the
reader. How do they:

- use topic sentences?
- connect active writing sentences
  back to the topic sentence?
- join one paragraph to another?

Write out some of the paragraphs,
and display them with labels to show
how paragraphing works.

ACTIVE READING
Paragraph structure in instructions

Giving clear instructions is an important skill. Paragraphs help us to organize ideas on similar topics. Writers often use other features to add clarity – for example, subheadings.

These are part of the instructions from one of *Blue Peter's* most famous 'makes' – 'How to make Tracy Island'. Explore the way paragraph features are used to give instructions.

Tracy Island

From the side of a large grocery carton – draw an oblong shape with three corners rounded off and the fourth slightly jutting out to make a runway for Thunderbird 2. Cut it out making the edges wavy to give a natural looking island coastline. **A**

A soap powder packet makes a perfect secret cave which is Thunderbird 2's hangar. Cut away the flaps at one end. Cut away the other end at a sloping angle so it fits the back of the base, facing the runway. Check you've left enough runway for

Thunderbird 2 before fixing the box in place with sticky tape. **B**

The Lookout is made from a cream cheese box with one half painted grey. Keep the lid on one side. **C**

Fix just the back edge of the cheese box to the hangar with sticky tape. Overlap the front edge about 3 cm. Remember not to fix the box at the front as the hangar door will slide under it later on. **D**

❶ Each paragraph has been labelled A to D. For each paragraph, write down what the main topic is.

❷ How did you work out what the main topic was? What was the chief clue in each paragraph?

❸ Is this a chronological text (arranged in the order in which things happen) or a non-chronological text? Could the paragraphs be placed in any order, or do they have to follow this sequence? Try to explain why.

❹ Many of the sentences begin with a verb: **cut away . . . fix just . . . remember not to . . .**
What sentence functions are these – questions, statements, commands or exclamations? How can you tell?

Active writing

Look at these comments on the instructions:

'These instructions could be set out in different ways. For example, if each step in the process was numbered they would be even clearer. One way of making the information simple to follow would be to place the instructions in one column, with tips and advice separately in another column. Illustrations would be best of all.'

Do you agree?

Take the *Blue Peter* text and experiment with different ways of setting out the instructions, ensuring that they are clear and simple to use. Present them on a side of A4 paper.

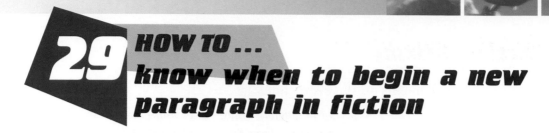

29 HOW TO ...
know when to begin a new paragraph in fiction

Exploring language

Activity 1

Read this story outline. If you were writing the story, where would you begin new paragraphs?

A car is driving along a deserted road near the sea. **A** A foghorn sounds. **B** The driver becomes nervous and locks the doors and turns the radio up louder. **C** Out at sea a small fishing-boat is making its way back to shore. **D** It is later than expected and it is struggling against the tide. **E** The skipper makes towards the lighthouse. **F** Underneath the water a large creature wakes up. **G** The car driver feels sleepy and pulls in to rest. **H** The skipper of the boat worries that they aren't going to make it before midnight. **I** The creature begins to swim towards the surface. **J**

Use the letters **A** to **J** to show where you would begin new paragraphs.

Activity 2

Compare your paragraphing with a friend's. If you have made different decisions, explain why.

Activity 3

Based on Activities 1 and 2, complete these sentences:

◆ New paragraphs are essential to show the reader . . .
◆ You do not need to begin a new paragraph when . . .
◆ In stories, the most important time to use new paragraphs is when . . .

Activity 4 Which of these statements do you . . .

a strongly agree with
b generally agree with
c disagree with?

1 New paragraphs are a matter of personal choice.
2 Long paragraphs help the reader to get into the story.
3 You should start a new paragraph when you describe a different character.
4 You should start a new paragraph when you move forwards or backwards in time.
5 You should start a new paragraph when you change the viewpoint (e.g. from one character's view to another).

Activity 5 Where would you begin new paragraphs in this extract from a short story?

Goldilocks set off on her morning walk. On the other side of the forest the bears were about to begin breakfast. 'Ouch,' yelled Baby Bear, 'this porridge is far too hot.' 'Calm down, dear,' said Mrs Bear. 'There's no need to get in a strop about it.' 'I'm not getting in a strop.' 'You are.' 'I'm not.' 'Please be quiet,' murmured Mr Bear, lowering his newspaper. 'I'm trying to concentrate.' In the woods a wolf yawned.

Activity 6 Working with a friend, compare how you have used paragraphs in Activity 5. How many paragraphs have you used, and where have you begun them?

Activity 7 What would your advice on paragraphs be to new users of English? How should they use paragraphs:

a when writing direct speech?
b to show different points of view?

Give them some hints. You could start like this:

A *When using paragraphs for direct speech, you should . . .*

Core knowledge

Paragraphs are useful in fiction texts for achieving a number of effects:

◆ a change of speaker
◆ a change of time
◆ a change of place
◆ a change of viewpoint.

Practising the skill

Activity 8

This text is a rewritten fairy story. The paragraph breaks have been put in odd places.

a Using the numbers at the side, say why each is an odd place to begin a paragraph.

b Decide where you would place the beginnings of the paragraphs in this story. For each, say what the reason is (e.g. change of speaker, change of time).

Jack

Jack and his mother were very poor.

1

They hardly had the money to survive. 'Enough's enough,' said Jack's mother. 'It's time we had a better lifestyle.

2

'We'll just have to sell Bessy.' In the barn, Bessy's long ears pricked up. She thought she heard her name mentioned. Then she returned to munching dry hay. 'We can't sell Bessy,' said Jack. He was looking out of the window rather than doing his Maths homework.

3

'I've grown up with Bessy.

4

'She's been like a friend to me over the years.

5

'Remember that time she pulled me out of the canal after Rodney Fawcett pushed me in as a joke?' Tears were filling Jack's eyes. By this time the sun was warming the vast fields of corn. Birds sang loudly. Bessy shuffled nervously in her barn. 'We've no choice, Jack.

6

'She'll have to go.' Many years earlier Jack's mother had been comfortably off. Her husband – Desmond – and she had a pleasant life. Then the local landlord had increased the rent and Jack's father had gone further away to find a better job. Jack was just a baby. 'Stop being soppy, Jack,' said his mother.

7

'We've got no choice.' And so Jack was ordered to untie Bessy and lead her off to that morning's market to make a bit of money for the family . . .

Active writing

Use the story prompts below to continue the story, using paragraphs in the appropriate places.

Jack walks with Bessy to market. He thinks back to his childhood. He arrives in the square and looks around. A local farmer watches Bessy arrive and moves across. Jack and the farmer discuss prices (use dialogue – direct speech). The farmer offers some magic beans. Bessy looks on nervously. Jack accepts and heads home to his mother. Thirty minutes later he is home . . . and in big trouble.

After writing this next part of the story, draw arrows to each of your paragraph breaks. Then write a reason for the paragraph break – such as:

◆ new speaker
◆ change of setting
◆ change of time.

 30 ACTIVE READING
Exploring paragraphing in fiction

Different fiction writers use paragraphs in different ways. Some writers may use very short paragraphs, for example to keep the action moving quickly.

Others might use longer paragraphs, for example to develop a scene, description or character.

Read the opening of this novel by Ricardo Pinto called *The Chosen*. It is printed without paragraphs. Use the prompts to explore the way paragraphs might be used to organize his story.

All that day the wind had rattled the shutters and slanted the sky with snow, but in the warm heart of the hold Carnelian sat with some of his people around a fire, listening to their talk. **1** They were telling stories, the stories that those who could still remember told of their lives before the childgatherers came for them. **2** The words bleached his mind with the light of summers far away. **3** He settled back into the chair dreaming, his eyes narrowed against the leaping dazzle of the flames. **4** The tale rumbled on amid the whisper of women weaving, the remote clink and clatter of the kitchens, someone humming a song. **5** Behind all this was the keening wind which made him shiver, then sink deeper into the comfort of the chair. **6** A child's voice cried out, muffled, outside somewhere. **7** The spell broke. **8** Reddened faces turned from the fire. **9** They looked down the hall, between the pillars. **10** The great door opened and a girl slipped in. **11** A gust of snow-spotted air lifted some of the tapestries. **12** Carnelian rose with the others and drew his blanket round him. **13** The girl ran towards them, all eyes, breathless. **14** 'A boat.' **15** Her lips shaped the word with exaggerated care. **16** She stared round to make sure she saw the disbelief on every face. **17** She grinned, delighted to be the centre of all their staring. **18** Carnelian frowned. 'A ship?' **19** The girl looked up at him and gave a hard nod. **20** 'A ship, Carnie, I swear, a ship. **21** It's there, on the sea. **22** I saw it.' **23**

❶ How does this first sentence set the scene?

❷ Look at sentence 2. Could this work as the opening sentence of the story? Why or why not?

❸ Look at sentence 3. How does it refer back to sentence 2?

Active writing

A

How well does this opening work? Does it make you want to read on? Say why or why not.

B

Imagine this is the opening of a story for young children aged, say, 8–11. How would you simplify it?

You might:

◆ change some of the words
◆ make sentences shorter
◆ use short paragraphs.

Try rewriting the story opening for a younger audience.

31 HOW TO...
know when to begin a new paragraph in non-fiction

Exploring language

Activity 1

Read this short biography of US golf champion Bobby Jones.

Bobby Jones was first noticed for golfing skills when he won the US Open Championship. **A** He was twenty-one. **B** He went on to win three more US Opens, three British Open Championships and five US Open Championships. **C** In 1926 he became the first golfer to hold the US and British Open Championships at the same time. **D** His finest year was 1930 when he won four major competitions within five months. **E** During these eight successful years he also obtained degrees in English literature and engineering. **F** He also qualified as a barrister. **G** He retired from golf in 1930 and made some golf instruction films for a fee of $250,000. **H** He refused to become a professional player, but helped many others – including the young Jack Niklaus. **I** Bobby Jones died in 1971. **J**

Sort the paragraph under the following headings, using the letters at the end of each sentence. What topic does each sentence tell you about:

| Early career | Golfing success | Other achievements | End of his career |

Activity 2  Look at where you have placed each sentence.

◆ Does the order of the paragraph follow the sequence of Bobby Jones's life?
◆ Would it be possible for the sentences to be in a different order and all make sense?

Activity 3 Now look at this information about a golfing video. Look at the order of sentences and paragraphs.

Download this resource from the Active Grammar website

1 The 'Learn Golf' video provides information about how to teach children to play golf.**A** Although it is geared to the junior golfer, it can be applied to would-be golfers of any age.**B**

2 Through step-by-step lessons, you can learn about equipment options, the grip, the swing, how to take basic golf shots, golf etiquette, and methods of preparing children for competitive golf.**C** Other interesting golf instruction includes suggestions on which club to use at different places on the course and how to read a green.**D**

3 In 'Learn Golf', experts suggest fun ways to introduce children to the game, as well as continue to build their golfing skills in ways that are appropriate to their age and stage of development.**E**

4 The video thoroughly explains techniques and then demonstrates them.**F** For example, the swing is broken down into six basic parts including set-up position, posture, alignment, take-away, back swing, impact, and follow-through.**G**

5 'Learn Golf' is available on-line at £12.99.**H**

Could these sentences and paragraphs work in a different order?
Choose which of these statements you agree with:

Sequence of sentences within paragraphs

a All the sentences could be placed in a different order (c.g. C, then B, then D, then A . . .) and still make sense.
b Some of the sentences could be placed in a different order and still make sense.
c None of the sentences could be placed in a different order and still make sense.

Sequence of paragraphs within the whole text

d All the paragraphs could be placed in a different order (e.g. 2, then 1, then 4, then 3) and make sense.
e Some of the paragraphs could be placed in a different order and still make sense.
f None of the paragraphs could be placed in a different order and still make sense.

Activity 4 Compare your answers with a friend's. Discuss the reasons for any differences you find.

Activity 5 Look again at the first paragraph of the text:

The 'Learn Golf' video provides information about how to teach children to play golf.**A** Although it is geared to the junior golfer, it can be applied to would-be golfers of any age.**B**

1 How would you describe the **purpose** of sentence **A**?

2 Which of these descriptions best describes sentence **B**?
   a It adds more detail.
   b It introduces a new topic.
   c It clarifies sentence **A**.

3 What clue is there in sentence **B** that it is referring back to sentence **A**?

Activity 6 Now look again at sentence **C**:

Through step-by-step lessons, you can learn about equipment options, the grip, the swing, how to take basic golf shots, golf etiquette, and methods of preparing children for competitive golf.**C**

Do you think this needs to be in a separate paragraph, or could it have been part of paragraph 1?

Discuss what your group thinks. Come up with reasons for and against:

Reasons sentence **C** *should* be in a new paragraph	Reasons it does *not* need to be in a new paragraph

Activity 7 Look at paragraph 3, which is one sentence on its own.

In 'Learn Golf', experts suggest fun ways to introduce children to the game, as well as continue to build their golfing skills in ways that are appropriate to their age and stage of development. **E**

1 What is the topic of the sentence?
2 Why do you think the writer has placed it at the start of a new paragraph?
3 Imagine you are the editor of this text. What would you do with the new sentences shown below – would you place them in the same paragraph as sentence **E**, or put them in a separate paragraph?

New sentence	Same paragraph *or* separate paragraph	Reason?
a Your children will love it.		
b The video also shows you some of the most famous golf courses in the UK.		
c These experts are all professional golfers.		
d At £12.99 it's excellent value.		
e Skills include: stance, swing, and direction.		

Core knowledge

In non-fiction texts, paragraphs are used for these reasons:

◆ a change of topic
◆ to make a new point within a topic
◆ a change of time
◆ a change of viewpoint.

Paragraphs will usually start with a topic sentence. This is the sentence that gives the broadest information. The following sentences may then:

◆ add more information
◆ explain the topic sentence
◆ clarify points
◆ give examples.

Practising the skill

Activity 8

Look at this news story from the Newsround website. Using the table below, decide where the paragraph breaks should be and then give a reason, choosing from the list given.

Thursday
20th July 2000

South African teenager in shark attack

Teenager Shannon Ainslie was lucky to escape with only an injured right hand after a four-metre (13 ft) Great White shark attacked him whilst he was surfing.**1** The 15-year-old had been surfing in the Indian Ocean off South Africa's Sunshine Coast when he found himself staring right into the shark's eyes.**2** 'I was heading for a wave, all of a sudden a Great White shark about four metres grabbed me and the next minute I was underneath the water and I looked at the shark face to face.'**3** 'It suddenly let go of me so I grabbed my board.**4** I warned everybody else about the shark and said get out there is a shark in the water,' Shannon told reporters.**5** The shark had bitten into his hand, cutting through to the bone and leaving him unable to use it, but with only his left hand he was able to ride a wave back to shore where friends helped by tying a cord around his arm to stop the wound bleeding.**6** Great White sharks can grow up to seven metres or 21 feet and are found off the South African, Australian and Californian coasts.**7** Sharks do not usually attack humans nor do they eat us – they generally feed on seals and fish.**8** Some experts say that sharks attack people only when they have mistaken them for a seal.**9** In Shannon's case the shark may have mistaken his surf board for a large fish.**10**

Sentence	Start of new paragraph – Yes or No	If yes, reason: **a** change of topic **b** new point within topic **c** change of speaker **d** change of viewpoint **e** change of writing style **f** other reason
1		
2		
3		
4		
5		
6		
7		
8		
9		
10		

Activity 9 If you were asked to produce a summarized version of this text in just three sentences, which sentences would you use? Why?

Active writing

Choose one of the topics below. As quickly as you can, write down everything you know about the topic. Write as much as you can. Don't use paragraphs.

Topics:

- ◆ A band or singer you like
- ◆ A game or sport you know well
- ◆ A description of a film you have seen several times.

Then swap texts with a friend. Read the text through and organize it into paragraphs. Write it out – or edit it on screen – and then label the text to show:

- ◆ the topic sentences that start each paragraph
- ◆ how you decided where to begin each new paragraph (e.g. new information, new viewpoint, . . . and so on).

32 ACTIVE READING
Paragraphs in a book review

Book reviews give you someone's opinion about a text. They don't need to be written in any special order, but quite often they do tell you part of a book's storyline.

In this article from a fiction website, writer Shannon Maughan writes about *Harry Potter and the Goblet of Fire*. The article has been reprinted in the wrong order.

Un-jumble the paragraphs, using the letters **A** to **G** to indicate the order you would place it in. Then use the grid on the next page to explain why you have made your decisions.

A Yes, this is a very long book. But you'll want to step right into the enchanting world of Hogwarts and ride along as Harry unravels more of the magical mysteries in his fascinating life.

B Once at Hogwarts, though, Harry – and everyone else – gets a big surprise. They learn that Quidditch is cancelled for the year so that the school can concentrate on a different competition, the Triwizard Tournament. It's a contest between the three largest European schools of wizardry: Hogwarts, Beauxbatons, and Durmstrang. One champion is chosen to represent each school in a series of dangerous tasks. As students from the other two schools arrive to spend the year at Hogwarts, everyone wonders which students will compete, their names finally selected by the ancient Goblet of Fire.

C With two weeks of summer to go before school starts, Harry is thrilled to learn that he'll be leaving his wretched relatives, the Dursleys, and going to stay with his best friend, Ron Weasley, and Ron's family. But even more special than his visit is the chance to attend the Quidditch World Cup championship game. Harry, Ron, their friend Hermione, and most of the Weasley clan head off to a magical stadium for the big game. During all the festivities, the Dark Mark of Voldemort is raised in the sky, frightening the thousands of wizards and witches at the event. Could Voldemort be regaining his strength?

D He's baaaaaack! Harry Potter, boy wizard, returns in this much-anticipated fourth book about the amazing goings-on at Hogwarts School of Witchcraft and Wizardry.

E The Tournament is exciting, but it's only part of the year's activities. A regular class load, including instruction from Mad-Eye Moody, the new Defence Against the Dark Arts teacher with a magical eye and wooden leg, keeps Harry and his friends busy. Of course, there's time for fun, including weekend trips to the wizarding village of Hogsmeade. And at 14, Harry and his fellow fourth-years are ready for their first school dance (who will Harry ask?).

F Harry doesn't have too much time to worry about this scary idea as his fourth year at Hogwarts is about to begin. He may not be all that eager to start his school work, but he's super excited about the new Quidditch season. And he also wants to know who the new Defense Against the Dark Arts teacher will be.

G As the Triwizard Tournament and the school year unfold, nearly all the witchcraft and wizardry students face new challenges. But this year Harry faces the most danger of all. He now must trust that his growing wizard skills and the support of Professor Dumbledore, and his godfather, Sirius Black, will be enough to see Harry safely through this fourth year.

Shannon Maughan

Order	Paragraph letter A–G	Main clue about why it goes in this order
1		
2		
3		
4		
5		
6		
7		

Clues might include:

◆ use of topic sentence
◆ pronouns referring back to earlier references
◆ paragraphs introducing or summarizing material
◆ paragraphs telling part of the story.

33 HOW TO ...
use the first sentence to orientate the reader in the new paragraph

Exploring language

Activity 1 Look at these first sentences of paragraphs, taken from a range of sources. Some are from fiction and some are from non fiction texts. For each opening sentence, decide whether you think it is from a fiction or non-fiction text.

a Derby night at White City was hot with atmosphere as the crowd took their places.

b Five shepherds fell asleep under a tree.

c If you were to meet an Englishman in the year 1000, the first thing you could notice would be how tall he was – very much the size of anyone alive today.

d The funfair had closed for the night as Jake began his long walk home.

e Taking photographs can be a very satisfying way of capturing the happiest or most important times of your life.

Activity 2 Discuss the clues that told you whether the sentence was from a fiction or non-fiction text. For which sentences was it difficult to decide? Why?

Activity 3 Look at this list of fiction and non-fiction genres. Try to link each of the sentences in Activity 1 to one genre. Discuss this with a friend.

Fiction	Non-fiction
Legend, adventure story, horror story, historical novel, suspense story, detective fiction, comic novel	Autobiography, travel writing, history book, sports writing, set of instructions, instruction leaflet, essay, newspaper article

Activity 4  For each of your answers in Activity 3, identify the main clue that helped you link the sentence to the genre. The main clue might be:

◆ a word or phrase
◆ a grammatical pattern.

34 ACTIVE READING
Exploring topic sentences in newspapers

Newspaper articles use a number of language and layout features to help the reader gain information as quickly as possible.

The topic sentence aims to tell the reader the whole story – including details about *who*, *what happened*, *where*, and *when*.

Read these openings from two news sources, and use the questions to explore the way they inform the reader.

❶ The first text is from the *Daily Mirror*. Look at the topic sentence. What does it tell you about:
who?
what happened?
when?
where?

❷ Look more closely at the headline. Before you even read the topic sentence, the headline gives you clues about the story. What clues does it give about what the story is about, and whether it is a serious or a flippant story?

❸ How does the newspaper use capital letters to add emphasis to the story?

A
IT'S NUT MY DAY

A SQUIRREL sparked an emergency when he got vertigo after climbing a 100ft building.

Office workers called the fire brigade after they spotted him clinging to the wall for over FOUR hours.

Daily Mirror, 22.9.00

B
Wednesday, 20 September, 2000, 13:33 GMT 14:33 UK

Narnia's magical revival

Classic children's fantasy book *The Lion, The Witch and The Wardrobe* is to be re-launched with a huge marketing campaign, capitalizing on the massive interest generated by the Harry Potter craze.

❹ Now look at text B, which comes from the BBC website. Look at the topic sentence. What does it tell you about:
what?
who?
when?
where?

❺ What clues can you find that this text was written for a different audience from text A?

❻ Topic sentences in newspapers use a lot of **modification** to pack in details about nouns and verbs. Write down the words used in extract B to modify these nouns:
- *book*
- *campaign*
- *craze*

Active writing

a Think of another title for text A.
b Think of a more entertaining topic sentence for text A.
c Rewrite text B, removing most or all of the modifiers.
d How is the text now different?

35 HOW TO ...
organize sentences within paragraphs

Exploring language

Activity 1

Read these four sentences. They are all taken from one paragraph, but here they have been jumbled up.
Try to work out what kind of text they come from.

A But like many children's books these days, the Harry Potter series has recently come under fire.

B In Minnesota, Michigan, New York, California, and South Carolina, parents who feel the books promote interest in the occult have called for their removal from classrooms and school libraries.

C Most of us think so.

D It's a good thing when children enjoy books, isn't it?

Finish these comments:

1 This text is about   (name a topic).
2 It is probably taken from a
   (name a text type, e.g. novel, biography, newspaper).
3 The purpose of the writing could be to   (name a purpose).

Activity 2

The four sentences are in the wrong order. Which do you think is the first sentence of the paragraph?

Use the grid below to explore the reasons:

Sentence	is / is not the first sentence	because . . .
Sentence A		
Sentence B		
Sentence C		
Sentence D		

Activity 3

Discuss the order in which you think the sentences should appear within the paragraph.

Which was easiest, and which the hardest to place? Why, do you think?

Use the activities below to explore each sentence a little more.

Activity 9
Write a paragraph using the notes below. They are probably not in the order you will want to use in your paragraph.

The early days of radio
◆ Transistors meant radios got much smaller in the 1940s.
◆ First radio broadcast: 1920.
◆ It was on 12 June.
◆ Dame Nellie Melba performed some opera.
◆ The first aerials were huge – around 10 by 20 metres.
◆ Radios became much more popular then.

Write this as an informative paragraph in your own words. Make sure your paragraph is clearly structured, using pronouns, conjunctions and linking words.

Activity 10
Use labels and arrows to demonstrate how you have constructed your paragraph in Activity 9. Use the labels below to explain your methods:

◆ topic sentence
◆ sentence adding detail
◆ conjunction
◆ pronoun referring back to the main topic
◆ linking words.

Active writing

A

Find five opening paragraphs from different non-fiction texts and compare the way the writers organize them. Look for:

◆ topic sentences
◆ linking features.

B

Choose one paragraph and label the writer's techniques.

C

Produce a handout or poster to show how to write successful paragraphs.

36 ACTIVE READING
Exploring paragraphing in newspapers

Newspapers often use short paragraphs. This helps the reader to pick up information quickly, starting with the overall story in the first paragraph, and then gaining more detail in later paragraphs.

Newspapers use other features to add clarity – such as headlines and subheadings.

Here are three newspapers reports on British athlete Jonathan Edwards's success in the 2000 Olympics.

❶ Look at the three headlines. Which do you think is
a most informative
b most jokey
c most successful?

❷ Look at the first paragraph of each text. Write down the subject of the topic sentence that begins each one.

❸ Journalism often uses **modification** to compress a lot of information into sentences (e.g. *frail pensioner Philippa Nettleton, 97*). Look at the first paragraph of text B. How does the writer use labels to describe Jonathan Edwards?

❹ Choose one text and look at the way the writer links paragraphs. Look for the use of pronouns (*he, it, they*); conjunctions (*and, although, but*); linking phrases (*later, earlier*).

❺ Compare and evaluate the three texts. Which is:
a most informative?
b most detailed?
c most emotional?
d most detached (unemotional)?
e most clear?
• Back up your answers with specific examples.

A

Edwards adds to gold rush
Special report: the Sydney Olympics

Vivek Chaudhary in Sydney
Tuesday September 26, 2000

An Olympic crowd of just over 112,000, the largest in the history of the modern games, witnessed another successful night for Great Britain, the highlight of which was a gold medal for Jonathan Edwards in the triple jump.

Edwards, whose mother-in-law died days before the games began, was close to tears during an emotional medal ceremony. The triple jump world record holder, who was taking part in his last major international event, won gold with a jump of 17.71 metres. Yoel Garcia of Cuba finished second with Denis Kapustin of Russia taking the bronze.

Britain won two further athletics medals as Olympic history was made, with nine finals on one night.

Guardian 26/9/00

B

OLYMPIC GAMES: TRIPLE JUMP: THREE STEPS TO HEAVEN

Edwards puts grief behind him with historic gold medal performance

GOLDEN boy Jonathan Edwards pushed Britain to an historic Olympic landmark with a magnificent leap of faith.

Edwards, a devout Christian, collected the triple-jump gold after revealing he had called on help from the Almighty.

His thrilling achievement ensured Britain celebrated its best haul of medals since 1956.

'I was on the point of tears on a number of occasions because I couldn't take it in that I was Olympic champion. It was almost too much,' said Edwards.

'More than ever before, I had a greater awareness of God's love for me and I felt I was destined to do well.' The gold medal came just a fortnight after Edwards lost his mother-in-law to a brain tumour, a personal blow that led him to consider pulling out of the Sydney Games altogether.

Mirror

C

Triple-jumping Edwards makes experience count
By Matthew Garrahan

With age comes wisdom and, in Jonathan Edwards' case, Olympic victory.

At 34, the Briton was the oldest man in Monday night's triple jump final but his third round effort of 17.71m was enough to see off his young challengers. The nearest, Yoel Garcia of Cuba, was 24cm shy of the winning leap.

Edwards has, more or less, dominated the sport since he broke the world record in 1995 but was unable to win gold in Atlanta four years ago.

Kenny Harrison, the Atlanta winner and Edwards' main rival over the last five years, failed to qualify for the US Olympic team this time.

FT.com

Jonathan Edwards celebrating his
Olympic gold medal

Active writing

What do we learn about Jonathan Edwards from the three articles?
Write two paragraphs for an entry about him in a sports encyclopaedia.

Think about:

- ◆ how you will organize the two paragraphs – what will the topics be?
- ◆ the kind of sentence you will use to begin each paragraph (topic
  sentences)
- ◆ how you will link later sentences to the first
- ◆ how you will link the second paragraph to the first
- ◆ how much modification you will use to give the reader detail about
  Edwards.

Word-level Activities and Reference

Words are what we use to label the world and express our ideas. We bind words together using phrases, clauses and ideas.

Words have their own structure too, and this section explores a few essential elements of words that will help you write more accurately and precisely.

It also gives you some rapid checklists which you can refer to when writing assignments and coursework.

This section:

◆ helps you to understand different uses of apostrophes
◆ shows you the difference between using apostrophes for possession and contraction
◆ explores the way we create plurals in English
◆ actively explores prefixes and suffixes
◆ adds a detailed glossary so that you can sharpen your grammar knowledge – quickly.

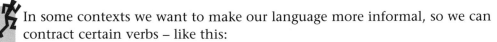

37 HOW TO ...
use apostrophes for contraction

Exploring language

Activity 1  In some contexts we want to make our language more informal, so we can contract certain verbs – like this:

I have = I've
It is = it's

What does the apostrophe (') tell us in these examples?

Activity 2 Make these separate words into single words containing an apostrophe:

1 Has not
2 Can not
3 There is
4 Must not
5 I am
6 Let us

Core knowledge

Apostrophes used for contraction can make our expression more informal. The apostrophe stands in place of letters that have been dropped out.

Active writing

Read these two letters and look at the way they use (or avoid using) apostrophes for contraction.

See whether you think each letter is too formal or too informal. Change the apostrophes so that the tone of each letter is right.

For each of the numbers, decide whether you would *change* (C) or *leave* (L) the words.

A Letter to a friend

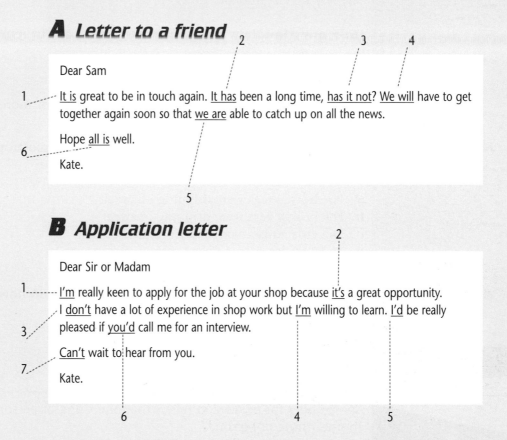

Dear Sam

1 — It is great to be in touch again. It has been a long time, has it not? We will have to get together again soon so that we are able to catch up on all the news.

2   3   4   5

6 — Hope all is well.

Kate.

B Application letter

Dear Sir or Madam

1 — I'm really keen to apply for the job at your shop because it's a great opportunity. I don't have a lot of experience in shop work but I'm willing to learn. I'd be really

3 — pleased if you'd call me for an interview.

7 — Can't wait to hear from you.

Kate.

2   6   4   5

The letters both set the wrong tone. They are wrong for their intended audience, partly because of the use of apostrophes and partly because of the vocabulary they use.

Rewrite both letters so that the style is more suitable to their purpose and audience. Then, for each one, write a sentence explaining the main changes you have made.

38 HOW TO ...
use apostrophes for possession

Exploring language

Activity 1 Look at these sentences and answer the quiz questions for each one:

The boy's teeth were bleeding.

Quiz question: how many boys were there – one or more than one?

The cats' fur was all mouldy.

Quiz question: how many cats were there – one or more than one?

Activity 2 Now look at these sentences. Look at the way the apostrophes are used. What does the apostrophe in each sentence tell you?

a The horse's legs were dripping in sweat.
b The horses' legs were dripping in sweat.
c The girls' knees were badly bruised.
d The girl's knees were badly bruised.

Activity 3 Based on Activities 1 and 2, think of a rule to explain how we use apostrophes for possession.

Core knowledge

Apostrophes for possession tell us that one thing or person 'belongs to' another thing or person.

It is important to think about where you place the apostrophe because this tells the reader how many things or people are doing the possessing – one or more than one. For example:

The **nurse's** bad temper = one nurse 's added to the noun nurse
The **nurses'** bad temper = more than one nurse ' added to the noun nurses

Pronouns do not need apostrophes, so they are simply written like this:

Theirs; ours; its

Practising the skill

Activity 4  The sentences below have their apostrophes missing. Using the grid, insert apostrophes at the right place in the noun – either before or after the 's'.

Example	Number
As a joke, I put on the dogs collar.	One dog
I smelt the neighbours dogs a mile away.	More than one neighbour
I watched the birds vicious attack on that sheep.	More than one bird
I ducked as the eagles claws got close to me.	One eagle

Download this resource from the Active Grammar website

Active writing

Design a poster giving rules for using apostrophes to indicate possession. Help students in other classes to understand:

◆ what apostrophes for possession do
◆ how to know whether to put them before or after the final 's' on a noun
◆ how to know the difference between its and it's.

39 HOW TO ...
use prefixes and suffixes

Exploring language

Activity 1  Look at the list of root words.

GLOSSARY

Root words

Words to which we can add prefixes and suffixes in order to change their meanings.

Download this resource from the Active Grammar website

Use the table to experiment with ways of changing the meanings of the root words, using prefixes and suffixes:

Root word	Change the meaning to ...	What do you need to add ...?
Happy	the opposite meaning	
Like	the opposite meaning	
Stamp	plural	
Stamp	Past tense	
Cover	Finding something	
Cover	Finding something again	

Possible prefixes
Pre-, re-, un-, dis-, im-, in-, de-

Possible suffixes
-s, -ed, -able, -ible, -ness, -ly, -ful

Activity 2 Choose two prefixes and two suffixes from the boxes. Write a sentence to explain how they change the meaning of root words. Then give an example, like this:

Prefix	Effect	Example
Un-	Makes the root word mean the opposite	unwise

Core knowledge

Prefixes are **morphemes** which are added to the beginning of a root word to change its meaning.

Suffixes are **morphemes** which are added to the end of root words, again to change their meaning. The morpheme *–s* or *–es* is added to many nouns to make them plural; the morpheme *–ed* is added to regular verbs to indicate past tense.

GLOSSARY

Morpheme – the smallest unit of form or meaning. Prefixes (e.g. *un~*) and suffixes (e.g. *~ness*) are morphemes.

Practising the skill

Activity 3  Look at the prefix table below. Imagine you are showing a new speaker of English how prefixes work. Try to write a paragraph which uses five of these prefixes.

Prefix	Meaning
Un-, in-, non-, im-	not
Mega-, super-	more; over
Sub-	less; under
Dis-, de-, un-	the reverse of
Mono-, bi-, tri-	indicating number: one, two or three

Activity 4 Look at this list of suffixes:

-ful
-ment
-ly
-ize
-like
-able
-ess

Write a paragraph which uses five of these.

Active writing

This is a made-up Mr Men story. The paragraph below has all the prefixes and suffixes mixed up. Write it out so that it makes sense.

Mr Mad was dehappy. He walks ofto the doctor's surgery and asked to see the doctor. Then he dismembered that he was reposed to be worker today. He quickness jumps up and got upto his car. He drove hurriedful to work, which was a megamarket. He noticing the replay in the window. It looked distidy. It was his job to reprove its appearness. Changed unto his megaform, he starting work . . .

◆ How many changes did you need to make to the prefixes and suffixes?
◆ Which were the most difficult to work out the original meanings for?

Write the next paragraph, again confusing all the prefixes and suffixes. Then someone else in your group can have a go at untangling them.

40 HOW TO ... create plurals

Exploring language

Activity 1 For most words in English we make plurals by adding –s or –es.

For each of these nouns decide whether the plural is made by

a adding -s
b adding -es; or
c adding a different suffix (or none).

1 the horse
2 the chimpanzee
3 the potato
4 the church
5 the fish
6 the sheep
7 the child
8 the piano
9 the family
10 the chimney

Activity 2 What advice would you give a new user of English. When do we add -s and when is it -es?

Core knowledge

- Most nouns in English are made plural by adding -s (rat+s, computer+s).
- If they end in s, x, ch or sh, we add -es – this makes them easier to say (rushes, sixes).
- If the noun ends in y, we usually add -s (toy+s, birthday+s).
- If the noun ends in y with a consonant before it, add -ies (bab+ies).
- If the noun ends ey, we add -s (monkey+s, valley+s).
- Many words ending in f or fe, change to -ves in the plural (thieves).
- Some irregular words don't change their form at all for the plural form (sheep).

Active writing

A

Read the following paragraph. The highlighted words need to be changed into plurals, using the rules given in the Core Knowledge panel.

Some **leaf** fell from the **bush** and dropped on to the **car** below. Behind the **chimney** some **thief** were watching. Both carried **knife** and had menacing **face**. They didn't realize that the **duty** of the two **policeman** on duty that night brought them past the place where the **burglar** were waiting. The police also knew that, concealed in special **box**, there were **camera** recording **video** of the area. The **villain** were not going to be **hero** tonight.

B

For each of the spelling rules about plurals given above, try to think of some more examples of words that fit the pattern. Write them on to large pieces of paper to display in your classroom.

ACTIVE GRAMMAR GLOSSARY

Active and passive	The passive voice turns a sentence around so that the object comes first and the subject is placed later – like this: The window was smashed by the burglar. The passive voice places emphasis on what happened rather than on who did it. The passive voice will sometimes leave the subject out altogether: The kitchen window was smashed. The passive voice is not very common in most speech and writing, except in some types of texts. It can be useful where the speaker/writer wishes to: ◆ withhold information at first ◆ conceal information altogether ◆ build suspense ◆ give emphasis to what happened, rather than to who did it.
Adjective	Adjectives give more information about a noun or pronoun – e.g. the **angry** horse; she is **horrible**.
Adverb	Adverbs give more information about a verb – e.g. the boy ran **clumsily**. Adverbs can tell us about manner (slowly), time (yesterday) and place (nearby).
Apostrophe	Apostrophes are used for two different purposes. **1** An apostrophe shows when two words have been compressed and some letters are missing (did + not = didn't). We use this type of expression more in informal situations. **2** Apostrophes show that something belongs to someone (Sarah's money). The apostrophe can inform the reader about whether the noun is singular (just one) or plural (more than one) according to its position. For example: I noticed the horse's bad behaviour places the apostrophe after horse to show that there is just one horse. I noticed the horses' bad behaviour places the apostrophe after the plural, horses, so that we know there is more than one horse.
Auxiliary verb	Auxiliary verbs are put before the main verb to change its meaning – such as to indicate number and tense:

auxiliary verb/s	main verb
is	eating
are	eating
has been	eating
will	eat
might	eat

The most common auxiliary verbs are to be (is/was/are/am/were) and to have (has/had/have).

Capital letter	Capital letters are used: ◆ to show the start of sentences ◆ to show the names of people (Jan), places (Oxford), and products (Apple Computers) ◆ to show the start of spoken words (within speech marks).

Clause	A clause is a group of words formed around a verb. Clauses are used to make up sentences. This compound sentence contains two clauses linked by *and*: The bullfighter left the ring and the crowd broke into applause. The complex sentence below also contains two clauses. One is the **main clause** (it carries the main information). The second is the **subordinate** or **dependent clause** (it gives background detail): The bullfighter left the ring, dragging his cape behind him.
Colon	The colon is a punctuation mark which introduces a list, quotation or statement, e.g. Please bring the following: a raincoat, some boots and some sandwiches.
Comma	Commas are used: ◆ to separate items in a list or strings of adjectives, e.g. The cold, dark night was approaching. ◆ to introduce direct speech and replace the full stop at the end of the spoken sentence, e.g. He said, 'Hello.' 'Hi,' she replied. ◆ to mark off a relative clause, e.g. The car, which was now repaired, moved off along the street. ◆ to mark off many connecting adverbs, e.g. Quickly, she hid herself. ◆ to attach a question tag to a statement, e.g. You do understand this, don't you? ◆ to attach a name when we are addressing someone, e.g. Hello, Mum. ◆ after a subordinate clause which begins a sentence, e.g. Because the weather had changed, we went indoors.
Conjunction	A conjunction is a word used for joining sentences and ideas together. The most commonly used examples are and, but, or, and because.
Connective	A connective is a word or phrase that helps us to make connections between different ideas in a text. Typical examples include: on the other hand; however; in fact. Each of these hints that the sentence or paragraph which follows will connect with what has gone before, giving a different argument – on the other hand/however – or adding more information – in fact.
Dash	Dashes are punctuation marks used to add information, or – sometimes – to bracket off ideas, as in this sentence.
Dialect	A dialect is a variety of English. Just as there are different varieties of breakfast cereal, some sweet, some healthy, some crunchy, some smooth, so English has varieties of words and grammatical constructions. The word hedgehog is used in some regions; urchin is preferred in other places. The sentence I will teach you that later is the normal way of speaking in some places; in others you might say, I will learn you that later. Dialects remind us of our roots – the way language has developed differently in different regions over hundreds of years. In formal situations and in writing, standard English is usually used.
Direct speech	A speaker's words or thoughts, placed within speech marks, are called direct speech.
Dynamic and stative verbs	Dynamic verbs describe actions (to hit, to travel, to jump). Stative verbs describe states of mind (to think, to hope, to be).
Exclamation mark	Exclamation marks are used to show urgency or emotion e.g. Get out of here!
Full stop	Full stops mark the ends of sentences.
Genre	A genre is a type or category of writing, e.g. some fiction categories include: science fiction, horror and crime writing.

Hyphen	A hyphen can join two words together (hat-trick means something different from hat trick). Hyphens are also used to show where words have been split at the ends of lines.
Inflection	Inflection is the way words change their shape to show, for example, that they are singular or plural (e.g. table becomes tables) and to indicate tense (e.g. change becomes changes/changed/changing)
Lexical and grammatical words	Lexical words carry the specific message in our sentences. When young children use **telegrammatic language** (before they can speak in full sentences), they mostly use lexical words: Car go fast. Grammatical words are the words that give structure in sentences: The ____ is ___ ____.
Minor sentence	A sentence which contains no verb is called a minor sentence. Exclamations are often minor sentences – Never!; Ouch!
Modification	Modification allows us to add detail to texts. For example, we can: ◆ modify a noun with an adjective: the **ugly** animal ◆ modify a noun with a phrase: the animal **in the car park** ◆ modify a noun with a clause: the animal **which I hated to look at** ◆ modify an adjective with an adverb: the **very** ugly animal ◆ modify a verb with an adverb: the house was **slowly** collapsing ◆ modify a verb with a phrase: the house was collapsing **before our eyes** ◆ modify a verb with a clause: the house was collapsing, **which I had first noticed** at noon.
Morpheme	A morpheme is the smallest unit of form or meaning. Sometimes a word will contain one morpheme (happy); sometimes two (un+happy); sometimes more (un+happi+ness). Prefixes (un~) and suffixes (~ness) are morphemes.
Noun	A noun is a word which labels a person, thing or idea. There are four types of noun. **1** Common noun: computer, sandwich, cats. **2** Proper noun: Pepsi, Russia, Sally. **3** Abstract noun: death, hunger, heaven. **4** Collective noun: **pack** of dogs, **flock** of sheep.
Paragraph	A group of sentences linked together by their theme or topic form a paragraph. Paragraphs are useful in fiction texts to indicate: ◆ a change of speaker ◆ a change of time ◆ a change of place ◆ a change of viewpoint. In non-fiction texts, paragraphs are used for: ◆ a change of topic ◆ to make a new point within a topic ◆ a change of time ◆ a change of viewpoint.
Parenthetical commas	Commas can be used like brackets (or parentheses) to mark off a clause within a sentence. For example: The skateboarder, who was an old woman, wobbled down our street. The sentence would make sense without the commas but, paired up like that, they help the reader to follow the meaning clearly.

Passive voice	See **Active and passive**.
Phrase	A group of words which makes sense within a clause or sentence but cannot stand on its own is called a phrase – e.g. the old grey overcoat; my garden; thinking carefully.
Plural	'Plural' means that there is more than one. In English, nouns are usually made plural by adding -s or -es.
Prefix	Prefixes are letters added to the beginning of a word to change its meaning (e.g. un+happy).
Preposition	Prepositions are used chiefly to show where something or someone is – for example in, on, under. Sometimes we use 'multi-word' prepositions – ahead of, near to, in addition to.
Pronoun	Pronouns can be used in place of a noun – e.g. The Prime Minister visited today. Did **you** see **him**?
Punctuation	The marks we use in writing to help the reader understand our ideas are called punctuation marks. They are the written equivalent of the way we use tone of voice and pauses in speech.
Question mark	A question mark indicates that the sentence is a question, e.g. What on earth is that? In speech, we raise the pitch of our voice at the end to show that a sentence is a question.
Register	Register means the way we change our use of language in different situations. We might use a formal register in a school assembly: Good morning, today I wish to discuss . . . An informal register might be used with friends: Hi, let me tell you about . . .
Relative clause	A relative clause is a group of words built around a verb, which can be added to sentences to give more detail. A simple sentence is: My dog is looking unwell. A relative clause can be added after the subject: My dog, which was four last week, is looking unwell. Relative clauses can be added at other points too: My dog is looking unwell, which is a shame.
Relative pronoun	Relative pronouns are words such as who, which and that, used at the start of relative clauses.
Root words	Root words are those that can have prefixes and suffixes added to them in order to change their meanings, e.g. happy becomes unhappy or happiness.
Semi-colon	Semi-colons are punctuation marks that indicate a break less strong than a full stop but stronger than a comma. They often replace the word and between clauses and phrases on a similar topic, e.g. My Mum likes my pet rat; my Dad prefers my piranha. They can also be used to separate longer items in a list.
Sentence	A sentence is a group of words which can stand on their own. We expect sentences to: ◆ contain a main verb ◆ begin with a capital letter ◆ end with a full stop, question mark or exclamation mark.
Sentence functions	Sentence functions indicate the purposes of sentences: whether they are statements, questions, commands or exclamations.
Sentence type	The different sentence types are simple, compound and complex.

Singular	A singular noun indicates that there is only one – e.g. desk, computer, telephone. These are singular. To become plural, each would gain an -*s*. Some words are the same in their singular and plural forms – e.g. One sheep; 20 sheep.
Standard English	The most important dialect or variety of English is called Standard English. It is used in most written texts, in education, in law, and in the media. It is the form of English defined in dictionaries.
Subject and object	The subject is the person or thing in a sentence that is doing the action of the verb. In Mary shouted at Kim, Mary is the subject – she is doing the shouting. The object is the person who receives the action – in this case, Kim.
Suffix	Suffixes are letters added to the end of a word to change its meaning – e.g. hope + less.
Synonym	A synonym is a word which has a similar meaning to another word. Synonyms for fire include: blaze, flames, conflagration. You would choose different words according to the register you were using.
Telegrammatic language	Telegrammatic language is a style that leaves out some words (the grammatical words). Children use this style when they have learned their first words but cannot yet speak in complete sentences. It sounds like this: Car go fast. Car big. The child uses lexical words (words that carry specific information) and leaves out grammatical words (words which provide structure within sentences).
Tense	English changes the ending of verbs to show the present and past tenses: She laugh+s . . . she laugh+ed To show the future tense, we sometimes use the present tense with an adverbial: The train leaves **soon.** The train leaves **in five minutes.** The train leaves **tomorrow**. We can also create future tense by using the modal verbs will / would / shall / might: The train **will** leave in five minutes. The train **might** leave in five minutes.
Topic sentence	A topic sentence is the sentence at the start of a text or paragraph which tells you what the content will be. Newspaper stories usually start with topic sentences telling you *who*, *where*, and *when*. Example: A 77-year-old man was dramatically rescued in York last night when flood waters threatened to engulf his house.
Verb	A verb tells us what someone or something is doing – e.g. She **saw** the car. It **slowed** to a standstill.
Verb phrase	Sometimes we use a number of verbs together to add detail, for example about tense (when something happened). This is called a verb phrase. For example: I eat – main verb I have eaten – verb phrase I will eat – verb phrase I would have eaten – verb phrase
Word class	A word class is a group of words which share a particular function in a sentence – e.g. nouns, verbs, adjectives, adverbs, prepositions, conjunctions.

Acknowledgements

We are grateful to the following for permission to reprint copyright material:

Gillon Aitken Associates for extract from Jonathan Raban: *Coasting* (Collins Harvill, 1986), copyright © Jonathan Raban 1986

BBC for web site article 'South African teenager in shark attack', *Newsround*, Thursday, 26 August 1999, and for 'Thunderbirds: Tracey Island' activity, *Blue Peter* web site, September 2000

BBC Worldwide Ltd for 'How to tell how old a raw egg is' from Delia Smith: *Delia's How to Cook: Book 1* (BBC Books, 1998). copyright © Delia Smith 1998

The Book Report Network for review by Shannon Maughan of *Harry Potter and the Goblet of Fire* by J. K. Rowling from Kidsread.com web site, copyright © 2000 by kidsread.com. All rights reserved

Alex Brychta and Oxford University Press for illustration of dog from Roderick Hunt: *Floppy, Floppy*, illustrated by Alex Brychta (Oxford Reading Tree, 1998)

Financial Times for article by Matthew Garrahan: 'Triple-jumping Edwards makes experience count', FT.com, 25 September 2000

The Guardian for article by Vivek Chaudhary: 'Edwards adds to gold rush', *The Guardian*, 26 September 2000, copyright © *The Guardian* 2000

HarperCollins Publishers Ltd for extract from Nigel Slater: *Real Good Food* (Fourth Estate, 1995), and extract from E. Annie Proulx: 'The Governors of Wyoming' in *Close Range: Wyoming Stories* (Fourth Estate, 1999)

Mirror Syndication International for opening of article: 'It's nut my day', *Daily Mirror*, 22 September 2000, and article: 'Three steps to heaven', *Daily Mirror*, 26 September 2000

Oxford University Press for extract from Roderick Hunt: *A New Dog*, illustrated by Alex Brychta (Oxford Reading Tree, OUP 1986)

Penguin Books Ltd for extract from Gervase Phinn: *The Other Side of the Dale* (Michael Joseph, 1998), copyright © Gervase Phinn 1998

Sainsbury's Supermarkets Ltd for extract from leaflet: 'An Easy Guide to Healthy Eating: The Vegetarian Way'

Transworld Publishers for extract from Ricardo Pinto: *Stone Dance of the Chameleon: The Chosen* (Bantam Press, a division of Transworld Publishers, 1999), copyright © Ricardo Pinto 1999. All rights reserved

Walker Books Ltd, London, for extract from Martin Waddell: *Sailor Bear*, illustrated by Virginia Austin (Walker Books, 1992), text copyright © 1992 Martin Waddell

Although every effort has been made to trace and contact copyright holders before publication this has not been possible in some cases. If notified the publisher will be pleased to rectify any errors or omissions at the earliest opportunity.

The publisher would like to thank the following for permission to reproduce photographs: page 32 Allsport/J. Squire, page 43 Fourth Estate Publishing, page 47 Oxford Scientific Films/S. Osolinski, page 54 Telegraph Colour Library/Planet Earth/J. Scott, page 67 Oxford Scientific Films/D. Cox, page 78 Fourth Estate Publishing, page 90 Corbis UK Ltd, page 96 Carlton TV, page 103 Joe Low Photography, page 104 Allsport, page 108 Bruce Coleman/Pacific Stock, page 116 Oxford Scientific Films/I. Cushing, page 122 Allsport/N. Wilson.

Additional photography by Oxford University Press Illustrations by Paul Davies

Special thanks to Sainsbury's, Witney, Oxon, and to Charlotte Brain